I0519075

EMPOWERED
YOU

Free Yourself from
Generational Conditioning
to Unleash Confidence,
Happiness, and Resilience

Praise for *Empowered You*

"Many people experience lives that are far from fulfilling, and they do not feel equipped or empowered to take the steps to experience the fullness of life. In fact, the richness of life is often unwittingly stolen from people because of events from their past, in particular childhood, where identity is forged and limiting beliefs are created, resulting in an inability to take action on the choices that will lead to an inspired life. In *Empowered You*, Phyllis Ginsberg offers a clear and actionable blueprint to free yourself from generational conditioning, unleashing your confidence, happiness, and resilience. By understanding childhood trauma and its impact, as well as gaining insight into self-identity and thought patterns—you have the potential to alter the trajectory of your life. Do not read this book. Study it, implement its lessons—and improve your life."

— Dr. Marcus Chacos, Author of *Self-Mastery*
and *The Arthritis Solution*

"Phyllis Ginsberg's *Empowered You* emanates a genuine warmth, reflecting the depth of her compassionate nature cultivated through life's trials. The authenticity in her words and the tone she sets make this book a powerful ally for anyone on the quest for personal growth. What sets Phyllis apart is her commitment to offering a buffet of wisdom, allowing readers to curate their own journey. It's a testament to her belief in empowering individuals to find what resonates best with their uniqueness."

— Emmanuel Dagher, Best Selling Author and Teacher

"*Empowered You* is a transformative masterpiece that delves deep into the intricacies of behavior patterns, offering profound insights into their roots. Phyllis' exceptional ability to identify the underlying factors and provide actionable steps for transformation makes this book a valuable guide on the journey to living an empowered life. A must-read for anyone seeking to uncover the layers and create lasting positive change."

— Vikki Rood, Empowerment Coach,
Speaker, and Author

"If you are curious about why you behave the way you do and want to make changes in your life, *Empowered You* is like an easy-to-read encyclopedia of human behavior that can help you understand yourself and what you can do to make those changes."

— Joie Seldon, Author of *Emotions: an Owner's Manual*

"*Empowered You* reinforces the principle that being true to ourselves is essential for happiness and resilience. Phyllis Ginsberg's work exemplifies the importance of authenticity."

— Mike Robbins, Author of *Be Yourself,
Everyone Else Is Already Taken*

"As someone who has delved deep into the roots of our sustainability crises, I've learned that the story we believe about ourselves and the world is the primary driver in human behavior. I often tell people that if you haven't consciously chosen your story, you are likely living according to someone else's story. Becoming aware of our childhood conditioning is essential in making any change, whether on the personal or collective level. *Empowered You* provides a roadmap for uncovering the limiting, corrosive stories we've been conditioned to believe at a time when we were far too young to choose and to consciously choose a story that will empower you to experience life consciously and freely."

— Chris Agnos, Co-Founder of Sustainable Human

EMPOWERED
YOU

Free Yourself from Generational Conditioning to Unleash Confidence, Happiness, and Resilience

PHYLLIS GINSBERG

Author of *Brain Makeover*

Copyright © 2024 Phyllis Ginsberg
All rights reserved. No part of this book may be used or reproduced in any manner without written permission from the author and publisher, except by reviewers, bloggers or other individuals who may quote brief passages, as long as they are clearly credited to the author.

Neither the publisher nor the author is engaged in rendering professional advice or services to the individual reader. The ideas and suggestions contained in this book are not intended as a substitute for professional help. Neither the author nor the publisher shall be liable or responsible for any loss or damage allegedly arising from any information or suggestion in this book.

Capucia LLC
211 Pauline Drive #513
York, PA 17402
www.capuciapublishing.com
Send questions to: support@capuciapublishing.com

Paperback ISBN: 978-1-954920-87-3
eBook ISBN: 978-1-954920-88-0
Library of Congress Control Number: 2024900506

Cover Design: Ranilo Cabo
Layout: Ranilo Cabo
Editor and Proofreader: Jennifer Crosswhite
Book Midwife: Karen Everitt

Printed in the United States of America

Capucia LLC is proud to be a part of the Tree Neutral˚ program. Tree Neutral offsets the number of trees consumed in the production and printing of this book by taking proactive steps such as planting trees in direct proportion to the number of trees used to print books. To learn more about Tree Neutral, please visit treeneutral.com.

Contents

Preface

By the age of eight, I could clean our 3,000-square-foot house, cook meals, and vacuum and rake the shag carpet that no one ever came to see. I was held to a standard of perfectionism by my mother, who wanted it done her way as she lay in bed with chronic pain from arthritis and migraine headaches.

When you are six, seven, or eight years old, you don't know what you don't know—and you get in trouble a lot. That was me, trying my best to "be a good girl" and do as I was told. I was taught to be nice, suppress my feelings—including my excitement—and do what it took to keep my mom and dad happy.

Needless to say, I didn't get to experience a childhood with family cohesiveness, support, encouragement, and the freedom to be me. Instead, I grew up afraid and became overly responsible as I did what I thought I was supposed to do while figuring out a lot of life on my own.

I came out of my childhood with survival skills—I could cook and clean—but relating to others was challenging. I spent a lot of time trying to find my way as I struggled through college and life. It's not easy navigating the adult world when you didn't get what you needed in childhood.

We all have had occurrences in our early years that caused us to live according to other people's spoken and unspoken expectations of us. It's the nature of how humans have been raised, and we learned to adapt to survive. The messages we heard during our first seven years got stored in our subconscious and continue to affect us as adults.

Generational messages about how we are "supposed to be" and what's acceptable, and what's not have shaped who we are today. Children who receive critical, judgmental, or invalidating messages are likely to become adults who develop poor coping skills and struggle through life. Messages from childhood, parenting styles, loyalty conflicts, and life experiences all play a part in who we have grown up to be. This book will help you understand the sources and patterns of how you became the person you are today.

As we replace generational programming, we will see and experience positive changes in ourselves and our relationships. No longer will our past dictate our present experiences. And when enough individuals adopt new ways of thinking, being, and doing is when we will see changes in our workplaces, communities, schools, and everywhere else!

Imagine living in an environment where trust is built and maintained, where adults and children feel safe, supported, respected, and valued and where we lift each other up with sincere words of encouragement. We'd be living as our best selves and encouraging others to do the same. We would be working together to bring out the best in each other.

I saw a photo on social media of a little girl wearing a shirt that expressed her view of herself, her feelings, and her needs. It said, "I'm not a naughty brat. I'm little, and I'm still learning. I get overwhelmed and frustrated just like you do. Because nobody is perfect. Help me. Guide me. Love me."

I'm here to lovingly help and guide you to nurture and support yourself as you learn new ways of thinking, feeling, coping, and being. Regardless of your upbringing and your current situation, you *can* create a more satisfying life for yourself. *You* are the only one who can change your life by replacing your early childhood programming, and that's empowering.

It's possible to replace the outdated messages we were programmed with and that are interfering with our ability to live a better life. When enough of us replace the messages we have been living by, we will collectively see a world where more and more people thrive.

How do I know? I've spent over thirty years working with adults and children who have experienced domestic violence, physical abuse, sexual abuse, mental and emotional abuse, neglect, rape, high-conflict divorce, substance abuse, and addictions. Personally and professionally, I have seen what happens when adults and children adopt new ways of thinking. They become happier, more resilient and empowered, more creative, and excited about life.

In part 1 of *Empowered You*, Limitations Created in Early Childhood and Adolescence, you will discover an understanding of how we got where we are individually and societally. Part 2, Messages from Childhood That Shaped Us, includes common messages and a brief look at current trends and historical events that have influenced us. Part 3, Becoming Your Authentic Self, is where you'll replace programmed messages, beliefs, and patterns to become who you define yourself to be. Part 4, Living and Working Together, includes what healthy relationships are and how we can contribute to a thriving world.

This book is interactive, so you will want a notebook or a journal to capture your thoughts, feelings, and ideas. Write down a few words on any topic that sparks a memory of an experience, a message, or anything that may be related to something you are dealing with in your life today.

I suggest taking your time as you go through each chapter. There are lots of stories, examples, bits of information, and questions to reflect on to help you discover who your conditioned self is and who your true self is.

Part 1

Limitations Created in Early Childhood and Adolescence

Chapter 1

Living Our Limitations

Scientists placed jumping frogs in jars with lids. These frogs were healthy, they had plenty of food and water, and as frogs do, they jumped and jumped and jumped, banging their heads on the lids again and again trying to get out. After thirty days, all the frogs had stopped jumping. They gave up trying to get out. On the thirtieth day, the lids were removed, and the frogs were free to jump out of the jars. But none of them did. They were conditioned to believe it was impossible.

Humans are not that different from the frogs in the experiment. Think about a happy baby, a carefree toddler, or a school-age child in awe of something they just learned. It's natural for children to have lots of energy and to be persistent about what they want. It is innate in children to explore their environment and to test and expand their limits.

Unfortunately, how most of us were parented, talked to, and taught in early childhood did not support our development to become confident, secure adults. Rather, like the frogs, we had limitations put on us in our formative years that caused us to become adults who feel unworthy, that we aren't enough or that we are incapable. As children, we learned our roles and our place in our family. We were told what to do and what not to do. And just like the frogs, we did not have a choice; we could not escape because we were dependent on our parents with no way of taking care of ourselves.

In the United States, when a child becomes an adult at eighteen, legally they are free from their parents. And for most of us, not much changes when we reach that milestone birthday. The patterns of limited thinking and ways of being have already been programmed into our subconscious.

I have worked with adults of all ages, including those in their sixties and seventies, who were still functioning in fear of going against the "rules" they were brought up with—and the thought had not crossed their minds that they, as adults, could make their own rules. That's how powerful the messages from early childhood are.

The root cause of what ails us as adults comes from the conditioning we received from multiple sources when we were impressionable, dependent, and powerless children. Messages got stored in our subconscious and continue to run our lives today. They are the basis for how we think, the view we have of ourselves, and the ways we make meaning from our experiences.

Collectively, we are all affected by traumas and tragedies. It seems that in today's world, people are more stressed, overwhelmed, and isolated than ever before. A staggering number of people are suffering from poor physical and mental health, poverty, homelessness, and addiction. A decline in the ability to cope and handle life is being seen worldwide.

Abandoning, neglecting, and abusing ourselves with substances, addictions, self-judgment, and self-punishment have become a way of life for millions of people. It's time for us to do something different so that we can stop feeling unworthy and stop retraumatizing ourselves out of fear and failed pursuits of trying to feel loved, acknowledged, and respected.

We have been the recipients of what our parents and caregivers had the ability to give us—which was heavily influenced by the circumstances they grew up in and the conditions their parents and grandparents lived in.

As you will see throughout this book, many of the struggles you face today can be traced back to childhood experiences and the messages you received about how to be or how not to be. No matter what you're struggling with, you can probably trace it back to something in your upbringing and how you learned to cope. Know that, for the most part, you have been living what you were taught and doing what you think you're supposed to or should do according to someone else's expectations. Your thoughts and beliefs were shaped by others through repetition, rewards, punishments, or threats.

The Human Brain Records Everything

Our brains are like computers, and they have stored everything we witnessed and heard in our early years. It is as if you had a video camera recording everything during the first seven years of your life:

What you saw, heard, and were taught—directly and indirectly.

What you were told about how to be and how not to be.

Messages from parents, relatives, siblings, friends, peers, teachers, community and religious leaders, coaches, and others.

By age seven, we made sense of what we had seen, heard, and experienced with others around communication and conflict. We learned what brought us attention and comfort and what got us in trouble. All of this is stored in our subconscious and continues to affect our decisions, actions, relationships, and ability to make and sustain lasting changes.

We function from our subconscious about ninety-five percent of the time. That means we are aware of only about five percent of our thoughts. Throughout this book, I will provide different perspectives so you can become more aware of your thoughts. Plus, you will learn proven ways to replace the generational conditioning causing you dissatisfaction or distress in your life.

Limiting Messages

Problems we struggle with today have roots that go way back. The messages we grew up with about how to be and how not to be have been passed down from generation to generation and shaped us into the people we are today. The way we live and relate to each other has been influenced by those who came before us and who lived difficult lives under harsh conditions.

The truth is that most of us function with significant deficits that prevent us from feeling good about ourselves and having the life we want to live.

Parents, peers, siblings, relatives, friends, teachers, the media, and society have contributed to how we see and feel about ourselves. We made sense of the messages we heard and made assumptions about ourselves. The most common conclusions we make about ourselves when we did not get the love, care, and support we needed in childhood are:

I'm not deserving.
I'm not worthy.
I don't belong.
I'm not good enough.
I'm not lovable.

What matters most about the messages we grew up with are the conclusions we made about ourselves, about life, and about how these messages are impacting us today.

We All Have Suffered

Even without an identifiable traumatic event in childhood, limiting messages influenced how we made sense of the world, our beliefs, and how we see ourselves. A child who is excited to share something with a parent that they can do, have learned, or have made has the desire to connect with that parent. If the parent gives disapproving feedback, is unresponsive, or is unavailable, for whatever reason, the child will stop seeking attention after numerous tries. This is a common conditioned response when an adult isn't there for a child in the way they needed.

Children make meaning of experiences when their needs or desires are not met. If there is a pattern of unmet needs, a child may feel rejected or neglected and conclude that their parent doesn't care. Self-doubt, a lack of confidence, and low self-esteem are just a few of the effects from unmet needs that cause so many intelligent adults to struggle through life.

Millions of people worldwide are in distress at this time in history. They feel depressed, overwhelmed, and that they don't measure up—no matter how hard they try and how much they want to feel better.

It's tough to get through life as an adult when we were raised with messages and had experiences in childhood that were disempowering and dishonoring of our strengths, talents, and who we are as individuals. These are the basis of our beliefs about ourselves and what is or is not possible.

Our mental, emotional, and physical health and well-being have suffered. Our relationships have suffered. The depth of distress can be seen in the substantial increases in anxiety, depression, addictions, and suicides. These symptoms indicate that what we are doing isn't working for us individually or collectively.

Life cannot get better if we continue to function from our limitations or from other people's expectations of us. It is time for a change and to remedy this problem at its root.

Life cannot get better if we continue to function from our limitations or from other people's expectations of us. It is time for a change and to remedy this problem at its root.

What We Didn't Get

Our parents, their parents, and generations before them did not learn to communicate clearly, confidently, and with compassion. We, just like them, learned to argue, yell, fight, threaten, punish, accommodate, back down, or shut down. We watched or were the recipients of these survival-based behaviors as they were being modeled.

Loving, caring, and compassionate parenting was rare, because for generations, fear and survival were what shaped parents' behaviors and abilities to relate to their children. Over the generations, parenting has been mostly authoritarian without much regard for children's needs.

Being Told What to Do

Adults do not like to be told what to do, and at the same time, subconsciously, they *do* want to be told what to do because it's familiar and keeps them safe. Another reason why adults want to be told what to do is so they don't make a mistake or a bad or wrong decision. They also don't want to disappoint their family, friends, or the people they work with or work for. The fear of not living up to other people's expectations is deeply ingrained in us.

The primary cause of adults remaining limited is that they are running their lives based on early childhood conditioning. Once you identify some of your programming, it will become easier to learn new ways of thinking and being that feel good to you.

Humanity Today and Concerning Trends

We have become a world of over eight billion people. We have access to endless information, entertainment, shopping, and the ability to connect with others at any hour of the day or night—and yet we are the sickest population (mentally, emotionally, and physically) that has ever inhabited the planet.

Fear and worry have increased, producing high levels of chronic stress, anxiety, depression, addictions, and suicide. There is a lack of trust in others as violence and hate have increased.

Events That Shaped Us

You might be wondering how we got to be a world so divided and destructive to each other and to ourselves. Because we were conditioned by messages from previous generations, we have all been affected by events that go back thousands of years.

Wars have been used to acquire or take "things" by asserting power, escalating conflict, and causing destruction and loss of lives. The Holocaust and the terrorist attacks on 9/11 are two more current large-scale events that instilled fear in the collective of society and around the world.

Historical occurrences impact the people who lived through them, influencing their lives in many ways, including their sense of safety and security. A high level of fear, judgment, and helplessness in individuals and societies has developed as others exhibited power and control over them. How we function today—how we think, feel, and act—and how we interact with each other have been influenced by the beliefs and messages of those who came before us.

Take a moment to think about the impact of events on your parents, grandparents, and on yourself.

Chapter 2

Challenges and Effects During Early Childhood and Adolescence

Young children are dependent, powerless, and influenced by parents, teachers, and caregivers. They have no choice about most of their day-to-day life, and they are barometers of their environment. Just as adults feel the tension in a room where there is conflict, so do children, and some kids misbehave, act cute, or retreat as ways of coping when there is tension.

Humans are hardwired for connection. Children learn to adapt and seek out positive or negative attention to survive. If a child does not have positive connections, they will subconsciously create ways to get attention by acting out or rebelling.

When a child's past experiences include being scolded, judged, criticized, threatened, abused, neglected, or severely punished in some way, out of survival they may emotionally shut down and disengage. Shut down children keep to themselves, spend more time alone, become less social, hide their emotions, and take fewer risks.

Children's Mental Health

Harvard University had this to say about the mental health of children:

> The emotional well-being of young children is directly tied to the functioning of their caregivers and the families in which they live. When these relationships are abusive, threatening, chronically neglectful, or otherwise psychologically harmful, they are a potent risk factor for the development of early mental health problems. In contrast, when relationships are reliably responsive and supportive, they can actually buffer young children from the adverse effects of other stressors. Therefore, reducing the stressors affecting children requires addressing the stresses on their families. (Center on Developing Child 2023)

Reducing stress in families is a good start, but it is not enough. It does not do anything to modify or replace the messages that drive the thoughts, feelings, and behaviors that prevent parents from coping and functioning in responsive and supportive ways.

Early Childhood Home Life

For some adults, their childhood was not a bed of roses but of thorns. They had fears and worries about things a child should not have to know about. A significant contribution to shaping who we have become as adults is from our early childhood home life. A young child may exhibit physical or emotional symptoms such as an upset stomach or an emotional outburst when worried about what is happening at home.

A child may not know specifically what is going on with a parent who is chronically ill or dealing with substance abuse, but they do pick up on it, and they may be put in the caretaking role of a parent or younger siblings. This can lead to inconsistent attendance at school or an inability to concentrate and learn. A child who is parentified at an early age tends not to fit in with others their age and may feel like an adult in a child's body, not knowing where they belong. As grown-ups, they tend to do what they learned to do—take care of others.

We Are Hardwired for Self-Preservation

As a child becomes mobile and expressive at one and two years old, they look to their parents and caregivers for feedback and adapt to their reactions. Because of how they were raised, most parents have a low tolerance for misbehavior and unrealistic expectations of their child's abilities to listen and do what they are told—often resulting in a tone of voice and words of dissatisfaction. Young children adapt and balance their desire for exploration and need for survival. This is how we all developed our coping skills. The negative effects of adapting to an environment in childhood that punishes or frightens us set us up to have relationship difficulties.

I worked with Marc, a forty-seven-year-old man who tearfully shared, "I have been in self-protection mode for so long. I keep people at arm's length. I don't know how to receive love. I don't think it has ever felt safe to be loved."

The Adaptive Child

When parenting includes severe punishment, threats, ultimatums, abuse, or neglect, the child must adapt to survive. Children who fear their parents are more likely to lie and to withhold information and their feelings. Fear and a lack of trust can develop in these children, causing them to become depressed, anxious, or outwardly expressive with anger.

When these children become adults, they tend to continue functioning from fear and a lack of trust in others. At home and work, they may lie to cover up mistakes so no one will find out.

Children raised to do what they "should do" and are "supposed to do" tend to work hard, run themselves into the ground, struggle, and put others first, leaving them with limited resources to cope, handle life, and have close relationships.

You may identify with some of these common fears of adults that cause stress and anxiety:

The fear of speaking up.
The fear of asking for what you want.
The fear of being misunderstood or not taken seriously.
The fear of judgment or criticism.
The fear of being seen as irresponsible or as a failure.

Discounting Ourselves and Feeling Inadequate

The result of non-affirming messages in childhood and adolescence includes discounting ourselves, holding back, hiding who we are, and downplaying our strengths, abilities, and talents.

Research has demonstrated that during their most impressionable years, children lack the ability to formulate a clear, separate sense of self. So, if our parents were unable, or unwilling, to communicate that we were acceptable, we had no choice but to view ourselves as they saw us—as unacceptable and inadequate.

If we were called selfish or told we were not smart enough, nice enough, or good enough, or our appearance was not to their liking, we came to regard ourselves as only conditionally acceptable. We learned to view ourselves negatively while internalizing feelings of rejection by critical parents, peers, and others. We came to accept an undesirable view of us as true.

Adolescents and adults who as children were frequently ignored, berated, blamed, or physically punished will somehow continue treating themselves in a hurtful manner. This is because of their undesirable view of themselves and the associated unresolved pain.

Sadly, most adults withhold kindness toward themselves due to their upbringing. Given our internal programming from childhood, we could not have behaved differently. It is not your fault for acting in ways that, at the time, you thought you had to to buffer yourself from anxiety, shame, or emotional distress. Or because you didn't know any other way.

Parent-Child Communication

A dynamic from childhood that gets solidified is parent-child communication, especially from birth to age seven, when communication tends to be one way: parent to child. We were told what to do, when to do it, and how to do it. When we become adults, that communication pattern is still with us. We get into relationships where we may take turns being the parent by telling others what to do and how to do it or being the child by adapting to what the other person says rather than participating in a discussion.

An example of this is when you are told to do something the way someone else wants it done (parent), and you immediately go to the thought, *I don't need to be told how to do it.* You may feel anger or resentment and want to speak those words but don't because it wouldn't be appropriate. That is the adaptive child in you who got triggered and had to suppress those feelings. This type of communication is common in relationships and work environments where a person has authority or is perceived to have authority over you.

Conflict in the Home between Adults

Can you recall how it felt when there was conflict between adults during your early years? It was probably scary, since most of our parents did not learn how to deal with conflict. It's normal to have disagreements. Since effective ways of handling conflict were not modeled in most homes, it is a challenge for adults today to navigate.

Children who grow up in homes with significant conflict or domestic violence have high levels of fear. Many of the children I worked with lived in fear of survival and what would happen to them and their parents. Their top concerns were safety, abuse, neglect, housing, food, and money. That's a lot for a child to worry about and carry into adulthood.

Expected to Be Independent

In Western culture, children are expected to grow up to be independent, self-sufficient, and work to support themselves. Regardless of how prepared or unprepared they are, they are expected to leave the childhood nest and function as adults in the adult world.

Since most children do not get the foundation necessary to become confident, independent adults, the excitement of becoming an adult and having independence may be short-lived when the reality sets in that being responsible for themselves as an adult is hard. Even with an education, it is nearly impossible for any adult to be financially self-sufficient with an entry-level or a minimum-wage job in today's world.

When we combine the complexities of being independent with negative mental and emotional experiences from child-hood, it is no wonder that so many adults of all ages struggle.

Part 2

Messages from Childhood That Shaped Us

Chapter 3

Messages That Shaped Us

Children absorb messages long before they can talk and make sense of what is going on. This is significant because what a child hears becomes the foundation from which they build an understanding of themselves, the world, and their place in it.

Parents' Good Intentions

Most parents have good intentions and may consciously parent differently than how they were parented. They set out to raise happy, healthy, and well-adjusted children. But here is what really happens. When your parents were children, they received messages from their parents about how to be and how not to be, what was acceptable, and what was frowned upon. These messages got imprinted in their subconscious by the time they were seven years old (just like yours did), before their brains developed enough to discern whether they agreed with the messages. Additional messages came from your parents' grandparents, other relatives, caregivers, teachers, society, religion, and the media—and these shaped their identity, beliefs, and outlook on life. Then they raised you with those messages deeply ingrained in their subconscious.

It is no one's fault, so there is no need to blame your parents or anyone else. They were doing what they could do—living from their own subconscious programming and the messages they received.

Generational Messages

I encourage you to explore this section as if you were a detective seeking to uncover clues that will provide answers to what is getting in the way of feeling or functioning better and creating the satisfying life you desire.

The following are common messages you may identify with from your upbringing. As you read the messages, it's normal to have thoughts, feelings, or memories come up from your past. Notice them; become aware of them. Your reaction will give you valuable information about what is stored in your subconscious that may very well be the cause of the difficulties in your life today. Most of these messages are universal and have been passed down from generation to generation for hundreds of years.

Now would be a good time to get some paper or a notebook to jot down messages you identify with and any others you think of.

How many of these historical messages did you hear during your childhood?

"Be a good girl," or "Be a good boy."
"Because I said so."
"Listen to me. You're not listening."
"Do as I say, not as I do."
"Don't be selfish."

Each of these messages have meanings.

"Be a good girl" or "Be a good boy" is a behavioral request not to be bad.

"Because I said so" is a message that discourages asking questions.

"Listen to me. You're not listening" is a message to get a child's attention to stop them from speaking or doing something they want to say or do.

"Do as I say, not as I do" is a message where words and actions have conflicting meanings.

"Don't be selfish" is a message to put the needs and wants of others first, or to share what you have, regardless of your individual needs, wants, or desires.

These messages may be well intended to create structure and to promote "good" behaviors that are acceptable in society. However, the way children make meaning of messages and internalize them stays with them well into adulthood.

Here are additional common messages that carry specific meanings.

"Children are to be seen and not heard" is a message of suppression.

"Girls are to be nice, kind, and helpful" is a message of how to be.

"Girls don't get mad" and "Boys don't cry" are messages to *not* express specific emotions.

"Wait until your father gets home" and "I'll give you something to cry about" are threatening messages.

"Why can't you be more like your brother or sister?" is a message of comparison and dissatisfaction with how you are behaving or who you are as an individual.

You may have made meanings of these messages in a different way. Your interpretation and experiences are valid. There is no one way to interpret these messages. The examples shared are intended to showcase messages that have been passed down for generations and to get you thinking about their impact on you as a child and an adult.

Historically humans needed to fit in and belong with their tribe to survive. As a communal species, we are hardwired to need to belong. Therefore as children, we often conclude that being seen or heard is a problem, which can lead to feeling like you're too much. As a result, you may have developed coping skills that included conforming and blending in to not draw attention to yourself. Conformity can feel safe at any age.

Can you see how your subconscious got programmed with messages that shaped how you have become? How you were talked to as a child—the words plus tone of voice, forms of punishment, and pressure to excel in school, sports, or extracurricular activities—contributed to how you function today as an adult.

Of course, children need to learn how to get along with others and act accordingly in various environments. With that said, the old ways of raising children are not working. I don't think they ever worked. They looked like they were effective, because in the past, children were raised to be more compliant and to suppress their emotions and needs. There was also an expectation to blindly show respect for parents, elder relatives, teachers, and authority figures—despite being harassed, abused, demeaned, disrespected, or misunderstood.

The Effects of Messages That Shaped Us

By looking at most adults, you wouldn't know they are living from their early childhood subconscious programming. For the most part, we are not aware of the impact this programming has on our lives and relationships. Mainly because we developed coping skills to hide the emotional pain, learned to live with it, and to look like we have it together—at least in public.

We came to conclusions about how to be and how not to be from the messages in our early years. The way we treat ourselves today comes from messages we got from those who raised us, along with experiences we have had up until this current moment. We made vows such as, "I'll never be like my mother or father." "When I grow up, no one is going to tell me what to do." Or "I'm never going to be in a relationship like my parents'."

Most of us were conditioned to listen to our parents, caregivers, and authority figures, not ourselves, our gut instincts, our intuition, or our bodies. In other words, we learned to be compliant and to override or suppress our feelings.

The messages we grew up with are the foundation of how we live our lives today until we recognize how they have impacted us. Then we have an opportunity to replace the messages that were invalidating, suppressing, and disempowering.

Ultimately, if we don't become aware of and replace the messages and meanings that shaped us, we will continue living by the subconscious programming that is running our lives, even if that is not what we intend. That's how powerful our subconscious is.

Chapter 4

Conditioned to Comply

Most adults are compliant. We do what others ask of us. We go to work and do our job, and we follow rules and laws. We may do what our friends, family, or partner asks of us without thinking about it. Why? Because we were conditioned to do what we were told to do in childhood, at home by our parents and at school by teachers.

Common messages that conditioned us to become compliant are:

"Because I said so."
"Do as I say."
"Do you want to be sent to your room?"
"Do you want to be sent to the principal's office?"
"What makes you think you're so special?"

The pattern of being compliant continues into adulthood unless we stop, question, or challenge the lifelong beliefs and expectations that were put upon us. Obedient children learn to do what they are told and will continue to live the way they were raised until becoming aware of what else is possible.

It's similar to the frog experiment at the beginning of the book where the frogs stopped jumping when the lids were on the jars, and after the lids were removed they did not try to jump out. We do the same thing as adults. We continue living from our conditioning long after our parents raised us.

Children comply for various reasons—to be safe and to be liked, and in most families, they obey because they are dependent and do not have a choice. Obedient children become adults who do not speak up, do not deal with conflict, and do not know what to do when their needs or wants conflict with others. Can you think of some of the ways you've been conditioned to comply?

Learning to think in terms of options and possibilities is not taught to most children. Limited thinking leads to an inability to do something different, to take risks and speak up when we have different thoughts or ideas.

Common thoughts and statements of people who do what they are told begin with:

I have to _____.
I should _____.
They expect me to _____.

It is no wonder so many of us feel powerless, angry, and resentful. Because we think we don't have a choice.

The Effects on Decision Making

Decision making can be challenging for adults who were raised to be compliant, because they did not get the opportunity to learn how to make their own decisions or they are afraid of making the "wrong" choice. Children who were punished, shamed, ridiculed, scolded, judged, or criticized for their decisions tend to shy away from making decisions out of fear. When presented with options, they may be easily overwhelmed and experience analysis paralysis. Obedient children grow up to become adults who fear the consequences of not making the right decision.

Brooke is in her thirties and had this to say about making decisions: "The pressure of making decisions makes me anxious. Sometimes I get so anxious that I avoid making any decisions."

Lori, a fifty-six-year-old woman who struggles with decision-making told me, "It's not okay to make a mistake. I second-guess my decisions and often wonder if I could have made a better choice."

Adults who fear making decisions give up easily or do not try to improve their situation because they believe something bad will happen if they make the wrong choice. Because of their fears, they can be prone to making self-sabotaging decisions.

Learned Helplessness

Another form of compliance is when parents do too much for their children. Parents who do things for their children that their children could do for themselves prevent them from developing necessary skills, which could lead to learned helplessness. Children who grow up lacking the abilities they need to function as competent adult—often feel helpless, stuck, and in some situations, hopeless.

Learned helplessness typically manifests as a lack of self-esteem, low motivation, and a lack of persistence, which can lead to the belief of being incompetent or useless. Learned helplessness is common in adults who have experienced early losses from death or divorce and repeated traumatic events, such as childhood neglect and abuse or domestic violence.

Identifying with Labels

Think of the specific comments you heard from others during your childhood. Did any sound like these? "You're lazy." "You're too much." "You're too sensitive." "You're so fat." "You're not good enough," or some other negative label. These labels can stay with us well into adulthood, causing us to conform, suppress our true selves, or "live up to" the negative expectations of others.

In childhood when we are told we are not good at math, cannot draw, or are not athletic, we form an unfavorable view of ourselves. When we are judged, shamed, or criticized for not performing to a certain standard, it makes us feel bad.

Sheri, age thirty-two, shared this experience she had when she was eleven years old: "I was embarrassed and humiliated when I didn't make the soccer team. At that moment, I decided I would never try out for anything *ever* again. As an adult, I don't try new things unless I believe I can do them. I have a fear of not being talented enough. I've missed out on many opportunities because of that one negative experience."

Unfortunately, children walk away from tryouts and competitions feeling bad about themselves when they are not selected or do not win. They make meaning from not being chosen and then label themselves as inadequate.

Children lack certain capabilities because they don't have much experience and are not emotionally prepared to handle the outcome. It's normal to feel disappointed when we compete and don't make it or don't win. Rather than internalizing shame about not being chosen or not winning, with the right support and encouragement, children can continue learning how to get better or find something else that more appropriately suits who they uniquely are.

There will always be people who are better than us at some things. With that said, if there is something you're not great at but you enjoy it, don't let competition or rejection stop you from pursuing what brings you joy.

Being Defined by Labels

We are defined by labels when we accept them as truth. Because of our upbringing that taught us to listen to others and not to ourselves, we easily take on labels from experts, teachers, coaches, and medical professionals without questioning if the label fits us.

Labels come in the form of what we have been told, something we have read about, or a conclusion from input about you. This applies to personality tests, quizzes, astrology, and general knowledge found on the internet.

Once adopted, a label often becomes our identity and a limitation we live by. Some labels may have a hold on us from a single incident, event, or comment, while others may be reinforced through repeat interactions. Whenever we call ourselves names or speak poorly about ourselves, we reinforce the label as our identity.

Influenced by Others and Advertising

Everywhere we look, we are prompted to do or be a certain way because of others' expectations and societal standards. We are drawn to do what is popular or common to satisfy the primal need to fit in. Historically, we have all been influenced to be obedient and conform to society, rules, and the expectations of others—of how to be and how not to be.

Because of our tendencies to internalize these expectations and influential messages, companies have learned how to effectively market products, services, and lifestyles to us, their consumers. Advertisers have shaped what we buy with promises of products that will make us more acceptable or more like those in popular culture or the media.

We have been conditioned through advertising to buy things we don't need, that newer is always better, and that we must have the shiny new updated version, especially of electronics, household items, and vehicles.

Social Media Today

Influencers, advertisers, and many people on social media post content that does not reflect the reality of everyday experiences. Videos, reels, stories, and photos are filtered, manipulated, or chosen to highlight an image that, for most people, is unrealistic or unattainable—be it a body image or lifestyle. The consequence is viewers feel bad about themselves, as if they don't measure up.

Social media is an open forum where people can offer unsolicited commentary that runs the gamut from favorable to critical or abusive. Social media has also become a platform where bullying of teens and young adults has led to suicides and where individuals often feel left out when they see their friends or peers having a good time without them.

Starting out as a place where people come together, social media now extends beyond "connecting" with others. It has since been monetized with advertisements and algorithms that do not foster connections as easily as in its early years. Instead, algorithms serve us content and ads based on on-site engagement and our buying or search history. Rather than promoting connection, the evolution of social media platforms has promoted overspending to attain a lifestyle represented by influencers, companies, and peers.

Millions of teens and adults are spending more time on sites that result in increased levels of comparison, shame, and fear of missing out (FOMO), leading to an overall dissatisfaction with themselves and their lives. This is another arena where people are highly, and often negatively, affected by others.

How much time is spent on social media sites? Total social media use worldwide in 2022 has soared from 90 minutes, or 1.5 hours a day in 2012, to 147 minutes, or two hours and 27 minutes a day (Oberlo 2023).

Chapter 5

Abilities, Accomplishments, and Celebrations

The messages you heard growing up about your abilities and accomplishments either uplifted you and allowed for celebrations or caused you to struggle with feelings of failure, disappointment, and denial of your successes.

Perhaps you heard some of these messages in your formative years.

Messages about Abilities

That's not how you do it.

You're doing it wrong.

You're so stupid.

You're not good at math.

If you can't be the best, you shouldn't do it.

That's just not your thing; move on.

Messages like these from childhood can lead adults to a never-ending pursuit of trying to "prove" to themselves and others they are capable. Thoughts that say we don't have abilities can leave us doubting ourselves.

Tom, a forty-six-year-old, couldn't understand why he kept procrastinating or why he would give up easily when things went wrong. It was from being told as a child that he was stupid and wouldn't amount to anything.

Messages about Accomplishments
Don't brag.
Be humble.
Don't upstage your brother, sister, or parents.
You haven't earned it if you haven't struggled.
What makes you think you're better than everyone else?

Adults who grow up with messages like these tend *not* to feel proud of their accomplishments and have difficulty celebrating their successes. They learned to downplay or not talk about their achievements so they don't make others feel bad.

Jackie, a highly creative woman in her sixties, learned to never feel good about anything she did because as a child she was punished for bringing attention to herself and her accomplishments. As a result, she has spent her entire adult life feeling worthless.

Penny, a woman in her midtwenties, told me, "I'm always playing it safe. I downplay my strengths and stay invisible so people in my family aren't jealous of me. Growing up, I was told not to do better than my older brother in school because it would make him feel bad."

Comparing and Measuring up to Others

Most of us base how we think and feel about ourselves and our efforts in relation to others, frequently by comparing ourselves to others who are more successful. Comparing ourselves to others can make us feel like we don't measure up, leaving us to focus on our limitations, inexperience, mistakes, and failed efforts.

We are often hardest on ourselves, unrealistically expecting perfectionism or to be further along than we are. We don't consider that others may be more skilled, proficient, or talented because they have been doing something much longer than we have. Additionally, they might have a natural talent or a mentor or coach who has helped them. A healthier outlook would be to aspire to be more like someone you admire and then pursue that path at a natural pace of learning for you.

Perfectionism

A desire to achieve is healthy. But an irrational desire to be perfect can cause problems when people hold themselves to impossibly high standards, thinking that what they do is never good enough. Perfectionists are generally competent people who look outside themselves for recognition or validation of their accomplishments. This level of competence often gets us more work, which can feel flattering, fulfilling the need to feel important, valued, or worthy and may come with financial rewards. Too much external validation can lead to burnout and reinforce the belief that we are valuable because of our achievements or what we do for others.

Perfectionism can diminish creativity, authenticity, and pursuing our own interests and passions—resulting in being overly cautious and missing out on opportunities. When given the chance to express themselves or to take a risk, a perfectionist will likely choose to demonstrate behavior that aligns with expectations or interests of others.

When learning something new, a perfectionist's beliefs and fears can prevent them from making progress and developing new skills and confidence. If it is too hard and a perfectionist does not think they can do it perfectly, they would rather give up to not risk failure. Reshma Saujani, the founder of Girls Who Code and the author of *Brave, Not Perfect: How Celebrating Imperfection Helps You Live Your Best, Most Joyful Life* (Saujani 2019), says that girls are raised to be perfect while boys are raised to be brave.

Perfectionism is a learned behavior. Children and teens are often driven to be overachievers in school where getting perfect or near-perfect scores is reinforced and rewarded, while "failures" and taking time to develop new skills are criticized or punished. Perfectionism also shows up in participation in sports, clubs, community service, and jobs. Perfectionism may lead to an obsession with success, yet it can interfere with the ability to achieve it.

Celebrations: Birthdays, Holidays, and Accomplishments
If celebrating feels comfortable, enjoyable, and easy, congratulations!

The experiences you had in childhood set you up to look forward to celebrations and being celebrated or to dread or avoid them. Celebrating can be complicated and bring up uncomfortable feelings based on past experiences and the messages we got about celebrating.

An accomplishment could make us feel terrible if we were brought up with the message to never bring attention to ourselves—as if we did something bad or wrong. Based on negative experiences, we may not take in our accomplishments, celebrate, and enjoy what we have done or created.

Then there are birthdays and holidays, which do not always go as we would like. I know this sounds negative, but this is the experience of so many people who feel neglected or disappointed and who tend to get depressed at times of holidays and celebrations.

For those of us who have difficulty celebrating, here is a list of why that might be.

What's the point of celebrating...

When holidays and birthdays are stressful?
When there is so much tension between us?
When memories of past celebrations are of conflict?
When growing up, celebrations didn't exist?

When perfectionism was more important than celebrating?
When you cannot please everyone?
When it feels foreign, and you don't know what to do?
When it's just another meal?
When you believe no one really cares?
When you don't want to be the center of attention?
When celebrations stir up painful memories of the past or triggers grief?
When you don't feel worthy or deserving?
When you believe others are jealous or envious of you?
When your family cannot be happy for you?
When you don't know how to celebrate?
When you don't know how you want to be celebrated?
When you don't know what would be meaningful?
When you are afraid of what will happen at a celebration?
When it's too much bother?
When you don't have the money?
When you don't know who to invite?
When you want to invite people who cannot be with you (because they are no longer alive, live too far, or cannot or will not come).

A negative association with celebrations and accomplishments can reinforce the need to deflect attention from ourselves. Often this is done by minimizing and hiding to avoid the uncomfortable feeling of having too much attention on us. It can feel extremely uncomfortable to be seen, appreciated, valued, and acknowledged if you grew up with messages not to stand out.

How we feel about ourselves is directly tied to the messages we got in our formative years. Negative messages about our abilities and accomplishments affect how we behave and perform and if we celebrate ourselves.

Which, if any, of the statements above about celebrating do you relate to and why? What would you prefer instead?

Chapter 6

Happiness and Being Loved

Happiness and love. Aren't they what we have been conditioned to seek? We see happiness and love in movies we watch and books we read. Everyone likes a good love story… And then there's how we live our lives, based on the relationships we saw modeled while growing up and the way people care and support or don't care and support each other.

Feeling Responsible for the Happiness of Others

In my work with adults, I often hear how they discount themselves and feel responsible for making sure everyone around them is happy and taken care of. Many adults were brought up to believe they had an influence over how their parents felt and that it was important to keep Mom and Dad happy.

Teri, a twenty-seven-year-old woman, told me, "I need to make other people happy. If they aren't happy, I don't feel safe."

Glen, a forty-three-year-old, described himself as a "people pleaser" who told others what he thought they wanted to hear so they would be happy.

Irene, a woman in her sixties, still feels responsible for others' feelings and said this: "Because of the way I was raised, I have fears about letting people down, disappointing them, or upsetting them."

Putting Others First

Sandra, age thirty-six, came to see me about her fear of letting others down. She learned to put others' needs first to keep the peace, making sure everyone else had what they needed.

Two common comments I hear when I ask clients about putting themselves first are: "I don't know why I can't be there for myself like I am for others." And "It's easier to take care of others than to care for myself."

A child who has been conditioned to put others first often struggles as an adult with their own self-care needs. And because they struggle in this way, they may be overweight or have a health condition due to an inability to put themselves and their needs first. Additionally, since they learned to neglect themselves, are not consistent with self-care, or cannot get themselves on a path to better health and well-being, it's common for them to feel bad and label themselves as lazy or a procrastinator.

As Gretchen Rubin defines in her book *The Four Tendencies* (Rubin 2017), an Obliger is the most common tendency, and obligers need external motivation to do things for themselves since they don't follow through with their own goals but will do it for others.

Adults who learned to put others first often choose jobs in helping professions because it comes naturally to them to help others, and that's not a bad thing. It is a problem, though, if you cannot tend to your own needs.

Looking Happy on the Outside

Rikka, a fifty-eight-year-old woman, shared this discovery. "I always thought of myself as a happy person, and when I look at pictures of myself as a child and young adult, I look happy. In my family, there wasn't room for me to be upset, angry, or needy. I learned to smile and hide my feelings, pretending everything was okay when it wasn't and pretending I was okay when I wasn't. I mastered looking good on the outside so nobody would know. I got so good at it that I didn't realize how much I was holding it together behind my happy smile."

For many of us, the ability to look good on the outside, despite how we feel on the inside, has been essential for our survival. And for highly over-functioning people, it has come at the expense of living an incongruent and inauthentic life.

The Reality of Happiness

Did you know that most people around the world are not happy? People say they want to feel happy, but few achieve it. A research team from the General Social Survey, which has collected data on American attitudes and behaviors at least every other year since 1972, reported that up until 2018, no less than 29% of Americans have ever called themselves very happy. The 2020 survey found that just 14% of American adults say they are very happy, down from 31% who said the same in 2018 (Associated Press 2020). Happiness will continue to elude us until we replace our subconscious programming from early childhood and give new meaning to how we live our lives.

Messages about Being Loved

As children, we learned at an early age that there are consequences to our behavior and that love is conditional. Conditional love is love that is given when we are good or compliant.

Many of us concluded that being loved is based on what we do, not who we are, and developed thoughts like these:

If I don't do what you want, you won't love me.
You'll love me if I do what you want or say.
I'm lovable when I'm good or do something well but not when I make a mistake or do something bad.

Additionally, love can be confusing when it's paired with physical punishment and a child is told, "I'm doing this because

I love you," as the child is spanked, hit, slapped, or abused in some manner.

Feeling Unloved and Unsupported

Children who lack enough positive connections where they feel loved, supported, and cared about may grow up believing they will never experience the love, support, and care they are seeking. Having this belief often results in a lack of faith, trust, and belief in others and in themselves causing them to:

Hold themselves back

Not speak up

Second-guess their decisions

Be indecisive

Feel stuck

Feel bad about themselves

Struggle through life

Have challenging relationships

Have unstable work

Experience financial problems

Feel lost, sad, afraid, angry, anxious, depressed, desperate, helpless, or hopeless

Feel stressed and tense

Have poor health

Cope by trying to get their needs met in unhealthy ways—like accommodating others, people pleasing, isolating, and numbing themselves with substances or behaviors like alcohol, food, shopping, work, or binge watching

Take some time to reflect or do some writing as you answer these questions:

What messages did you get about putting others first?
What messages did you receive about making others happy?
What effect have these messages had on your relationships and friendships?
What thoughts come to your mind when you think about being or not being loved, supported, and cared about?

Love Your Neighbor as Yourself

Whether you were brought up religiously or not, you've probably heard the saying, "Love your neighbor as yourself." There is an assumption that individuals love themselves and then act in a loving manner to their neighbor by being kind, considerate, compassionate, and generous.

There is an opportunity here to reflect on how you treat yourself, and if it's not very well, you are not alone. Millions of people are less than loving to themselves, mainly because of their upbringing and the messages they heard growing up about how to be and how not to be.

Can you see how the root cause of so much of what humanity is suffering with at this time in history is the result of not having enough positive connections and feeling loved, supported, and cared about?

Collectively, more and more of us are in distress from the effects of early childhood survival patterns that are no longer working for us. It is possible that we have reached a tipping point where we cannot or are not willing to continue living this way any longer. Genuine happiness, love, and care for ourselves are necessities if we are going to have authentic loving relationships and care for one another.

Chapter 7

Disapproval

Growing up we received far more disapproving messages than messages of approval. Messages about our mistakes, what we did wrong, and what we shouldn't do have profound, lasting effects.

The way we were talked to during our formative years set the tone for how we talk to ourselves and others, how we feel about ourselves, and how we conduct our lives.

Notice how you feel and what disapproving messages, both verbal and nonverbal, you relate to.

Messages about Disapproval
You're doing it wrong.
You're making a mistake.
You don't know what you're doing.
I wouldn't do that if I were you.
You can do what you want, but don't come to me when it doesn't work out.

Messages like these create doubt and cause children to become adults who feel unsure of themselves. They fear making mistakes, don't trust themselves, and in the back of their minds is the question, "What if they are right and I am making a mistake?"

Shannon, a woman in her forties, was constantly doubting herself. She questioned everything. She often wondered if she was making the right decisions about her relationship and work. She would ask herself questions like, "Would I be better off doing something else or being with someone else?"

The "Look" and Tone of Voice

How often have you internalized someone's reaction to you—a look, their tone of voice, or the words they said—and concluded they don't like you or you did something wrong?

Up to ninety percent of face-to-face communication is nonverbal, coming from body language, facial expressions, and tone of voice. A stern look or a disapproving expression sends a message, while an angry tone of voice may overpower the words being said.

Very young children interpret nonverbal communication with limited vocabulary and next to no communication skills. These early childhood interactions get imprinted and become the foundation for verbal and nonverbal communication in adulthood.

If you grew up with parents who came across as disapproving, as an adult it would be normal to think others disapprove of you too. The childhood pattern of believing we did something to cause a disapproving reaction continues until we realize there are other reasons why someone might behave in disapproving ways that have nothing to do with us. That person may be having a bad day, going through a rough time, or it's how they are because of how they were raised.

The Effects of Disapproving Messages in Childhood

An accumulation of messages has shaped us into who we are today. As children, we adapted and developed coping skills to survive. Based on what you heard and saw, you may have concluded that it was not okay to be yourself, to feel and express your feelings, and to have needs and wants.

Some of the traits of adults who grew up with disapproving messages are:

They are indifferent.
They aren't invested in what happens.
They don't have a preference.
They are willing to go along with what others decide.
They would rather let someone else choose.
They say yes when they want to say no.
They know what they don't want but don't know what they do want.
They live as if they don't deserve what they have worked for, earned, or achieved.

What traits do you identify with that are associated with disapproving messages?

The effects on children who grow up with disapproving messages are many, including the lack of ability to trust themselves, have a favorable view of themselves, or feel like a stable and confident adult.

They may also exhibit the following:

They often don't know how they feel.
They anticipate disappointment.
They have a difficult time making decisions.
They second-guess their decisions.
They lack clarity, motivation, and belief in themselves.
They are more comfortable following other people's lead.
They have a difficult time with relationships.
They neglect themselves.
They tend to struggle with their health.
They often feel unimportant, neglected, or abandoned.

What effect have disapproving messages had on you, how you feel, and how you treat yourself?

Those of us who were raised to be nice, kind, polite, and helpful tend to put others' needs first and function based on what we think we should do, have to do, are supposed to do, or out of obligation. Underneath the facade we show others, anger and resentment can build up that we may or may not be aware of. At some point, our suppressed emotions will surface.

They may catch us off guard, as we eventually express ourselves in uncharacteristic ways:

Nice people become angry when they have given too much of themselves.
Nice people become hostile when they can't take it anymore.
Nice people get sick when, over decades, they suppress their emotions to please others.

Chapter 8

Life, Work, and Money

In our modern society, money is a necessity, and the way to earn money has been primarily by working. Knowing our thoughts about life, work, and money is vital to how we approach where we spend a significant amount of our time and energy and how we live our lives. Early childhood messages about work and money can set us up to dread working to make a living, while the pressure to earn money can often make the primary focus of our lives earning money to survive.

A Historical Perspective

Two historical events shaped us as individuals and as a society in relation to life, work, and money. They are the Industrial Revolution and the Great Depression.

The Industrial Revolution (1760-1840) transformed society with the introduction of industries and machine manufacturing. It significantly changed the way people lived and produced a world where productivity is highly valued. This has led us to pursue doing more, earning more, and having more. There is nothing wrong with being successful and productive. Where it becomes a problem is when individuals push themselves to the point of exhaustion, live in chronic stress, or when they are out of balance with the other areas of their life.

The Great Depression was the worst economic downturn in the history of the industrialized world, lasting from 1929 to 1939. It began after the stock market crash of October 1929, which sent Wall Street into a panic and wiped out millions of investors. Over the next several years, consumer spending and investment dropped, causing steep declines in industrial output and employment as failing companies laid off workers. By 1933, when the Great Depression reached its lowest point, some fifteen million Americans were unemployed, and nearly half the country's banks had failed.

Both the Industrial Revolution and the Great Depression had a profound effect on our ancestors, with pressures and fears around productivity, job security, and an increased focus on money. Manufacturing and earnings became and continue to be the focus of so much of our lives that many view life as a grind. On top of having to work so much just to get by, the fear of not having enough money for basic needs affects many individuals and families.

The majority of our adult lives are spent working to earn money so that we can support ourselves to live. The messages you heard about having to work hard and not having enough can have a lasting impact on your thoughts and decisions about life, work, and money.

Messages about Life

Life is a struggle.

It's a dog-eat-dog world.

Life is hard, and then you die.

It's just the way it is, and there's nothing you can do about it.

These messages create adults who may strive for success and struggle as they compete for what they want, or they do not even try because they don't believe it is possible.

Barbara, a fifty-five-year-old, said this about her life: "It feels like no matter what I do, I can't get ahead." She wondered if it had to do with growing up hearing her mother complain about how hard life was.

Messages about Work

You have to work.

Hard work pays off.

Work before play.

Homework and chores have to be done before you can play.

You have to work hard if you want to make anything of your life.

These messages produce adults who tend to believe work is hard, not enjoyable, and something they must do whether they want to or not.

Megan, age forty-seven, puts pressure on herself to succeed. She has been conditioned to push herself—ignoring physical signs in her body from the stress of doing too much.

Victoria, a thirty-two-year-old woman, said, "I work so much I don't have time to enjoy my life."

Garrett, a sixty-two-year-old man, shared an "aha" moment: "I know exactly why I get sick—to rest, stop, and do nothing. Otherwise, I would just work."

Messages about Money
We can't afford that.
Money doesn't grow on trees.
Money is the root of all evil.
People with money use it to control others.
Good people don't have a lot of money.

Early childhood messages about money can create challenges in adulthood—everything from a lack of deserving and worthiness to how you view others who have money. A lack of money may spark feelings of jealousy or envy that could create an inner conflict when socializing or relating to others who are successful.

Jack, a thirty-six-year-old, grew up hearing the message, "Money doesn't grow on trees," when anyone in the family asked for a nonessential item. He could easily see how this message caused him to believe he would never have enough money, saying, "I have to work really hard just to get by."

Caroline, age forty-four, heard the message, "We can't afford it," so often that as an adult, her automatic response when thinking of buying something is, "I can't afford it."

Sally, a sixty-year-old, shared that she had been bad at managing money and felt embarrassed about not handling it well. She fears if she had more money, she would not be responsible with it.

Take a moment to reflect on or write about how messages about life, work, and money influenced you.

What were the messages you heard during your childhood and young adulthood about life, work, and money?

In what ways have you been influenced by the messages you heard about life, work, and money?

What effect have these messages had on your life? Job or career choices? Your financial decisions?

Whose Life Have You Been Living?

Did *you* really want what you have? The job, career, relationships, goals, lifestyle, car, clothes, etc.? Did you seek these out because you were taught or persuaded to want them?

Doing what you "should" because family, friends, or society says it will make you happy or is the responsible thing to do is common, especially when you were not encouraged to think about *your* needs, wants, dreams, and desires. You may have been discouraged from following your interests, passions, and dreams while being told you don't have what it takes.

Well-meaning adults who have "life experience" often give advice to be realistic or practical so we don't suffer from the same difficulties they did or make the same mistake they have had to live with. It's common to be told, "Go to college and get a degree in something that will get you a well-paying job."

In some families, young adults are pressured or threatened to do what others want them to do and become who they want them to be—or they may risk the loss of approval or financial support.

Rushed, Stressed, and Overwhelmed

Feeling rushed, pressured, stressed, overwhelmed, and working long hours. Does that sound like you? Can you remember being rushed as a child? Did you hear statements like these? "Hurry up, it's time to go." "We're going to be late if you don't get in the car now." "You have ten minutes to get this cleaned up, or else…"

It's no wonder that, as a society, we operate on overdrive and have so many adults and children with anxiety because of the pressure put on them and the pressure they put on themselves. This is not a sustainable way to live. Chronic stress and overwhelm takes a toll on us mentally and physically and can lead to burnout.

A rushed child may have self-talk that says, "I can't do it." Or "I can't get ready that quickly." Rushed children may feel anxious, especially if they can't walk as fast as the adult they are with and they lag behind. Rushed children become adults who put pressure on themselves, often feeling anxious and stressed or not smart or capable.

The anxiety a rushed child experiences can become a pattern of feeling that stays with them into adulthood and worsens when they feel overwhelmed or pressured to meet deadlines.

Over-Responsibility

Over-responsibility in adulthood comes from taking on too many adult responsibilities at a young age, such as caring for younger siblings, caring for an ailing parent, or doing most of the cooking, cleaning, and shopping.

Overly responsible adults are busy people who have overscheduled lives. They respond to others' demands and expectations, pushing their personal needs aside. They may work through lunch and into the night, rushing from one meeting to the next, fueled by adrenaline and caffeine, hardly giving themselves time to eat or go to the bathroom.

Overly responsible individuals often get taken advantage of by demanding people, desperate people, and people psychologist George Simon calls "covert aggressors," who manipulate others with flattery, guilt, threats, playing the victim, and superficial charm (Simon 2010).

They often use phrases like:

"You're so good at this." (A message of flattery)

"I'm counting on you." (A message of guilt)

"I really need you to do this." (A message of playing the victim)

"You're the only one who can do this." (A message of exaggeration—there are over eight billion people on the planet.)

Chapter 9

Sickness, Injuries, and Mental Health

It can feel awful to be sick or injured during childhood and not be taken seriously by a parent, teacher, or doctor. The messages we got in childhood when we were sick or injured determine how, as adults, we take care of ourselves or don't take care of ourselves when we are sick or injured. These messages also influence our mental health, how we treat our bodies, and how we cope.

Messages about Being Sick

You're not sick. You're okay.

You need to go to school.

You're sick again?

Don't be so sensitive.

Don't be dramatic.

These messages tell a child:

I don't believe you.
I don't have time for you.
You're not important.
I don't care how you feel.
How you feel doesn't matter.

Adults who grew up with messages like these about being sick or injured learn to override symptoms and carry on, ignoring how they feel. They may also delay seeking medical care once their symptoms get their attention.

Doris, a woman in her forties, told me, "I learned to discount sensations in my body. I don't trust myself when it comes to my health, and I put off going to the doctor as long as possible. All because I was continuously told by my mom that I wasn't sick when I didn't feel well."

Nancy, a fifty-one-year-old woman who works double shifts at her job, said, "I work through pain until I can't function. Having an illness or injury forces me to stop." The meaning she came to understand from being told she had to go to school when she didn't feel well was that she didn't have permission to stay home and rest.

What messages did you receive about being sick or injured?

What effect have these messages had on the way you take care of your body and cope?

Physical Pain, Illnesses, and Injuries

When we don't feel well, or worse—when we suffer from physical pain or symptoms that prevent us from carrying out our daily activities, it affects every area of our lives. We may have difficulty handling life, fulfilling our responsibilities, and managing our relationships.

In our fast-paced world where being productive is highly valued, it's common to feel run down and to override our body's signals to slow down or rest. For some of us, it takes an illness or injury to get us to stop and take care of ourselves.

When you don't feel well or feel uncomfortable, your body is trying to alert you that something isn't right. If you can relate to feeling run down, burned out, or frequently injured or ill, you might be reading this book at a pivotal time in your life and know that something has to change.

What that change is will be up to you. It may be a small change or a big change to nourish and take better care of yourself. You may benefit by carving out time for yourself, doing things you enjoy, or connecting with others. Or you may be like me when I had a back injury and spent a week laying on the floor. That's when I changed the direction of my life and decided to go to therapy school.

Body Signals

Children who were taught to ignore their feelings may also ignore the signals they get from their bodies. As adults, they tend to ignore minor aches and pains, hunger, thirst, tiredness, and the need to use the bathroom.

Thoughts that go with ignoring body signals are, "I have to get this done." "I just have one more thing to do, then I can stop, eat, use the bathroom, or rest." "I haven't earned the right to rest."

When you don't give yourself time to rest, rejuvenate, or feel your feelings, it limits you, and it's just a matter of time until your body gets your attention with more intense feelings or symptoms.

At some point in our lives, we will be faced with a physical or emotional situation that will be necessary to tend to.

Mental Health and Well-Being

Mental health includes our emotional, psychological, and social well-being. It affects how we think, feel, and act. It also determines how we handle stress, relate to others, and make choices. Our mental health can show us where we have areas of difficulty, and in most cases, the cause can be addressed. We can change thoughts that create anxiety. We can express unexpressed emotions and we can alleviate addictions.

We did not cause the challenges we have today. We were conditioned and programmed with messages that led us to believe and behave in ways that have kept us safe and able to handle life as best we can. There is no shame in feeling bad or struggling mentally, emotionally, or physically. It's not your fault. Remember, the messages you heard have been passed down for generations.

You have been doing the best you can with what you have been conditioned with and the coping skills you developed in childhood. And with that said, the generational childhood messages and programming we all have been operating from have led to an inability to function at our best, individually and collectively. Outdated messages have led us to live in survival mode and become a world of people at odds with ourselves and each other, resulting in not trusting ourselves or others.

Signs of distress from generational messages and conditioning include irritability, disgust, anger, resentment, depression, anxiety, lack of self-care, helplessness, hopelessness, yelling, lashing out at others, and an inability to contain emotions—all of these affect our mental health.

Thoughts, emotions, and beliefs can produce symptoms and feelings of stress, distress, and ultimately ill health. Mental health is vital at every stage of life, from childhood and adolescence through adulthood. If you are not sure if you or someone you know is living with mental health challenges, experiencing one or more of the following feelings or behaviors can be an early warning sign of a problem:

Eating or sleeping too much or too little.
Pulling away from people and usual activities.
Having low or no energy.
Feeling numb or as if nothing matters.

If you have thoughts, fantasies, or mental images about hurting yourself or have suicidal thoughts, get help right away by taking one of these actions:

Call 911 for emergencies or your local emergency number immediately.

Call a suicide hotline number. In the US, call the National Suicide Prevention Lifeline at 1-800-273-TALK (1-800-273-8255) any time of day.

Call 988, the Suicide and Crisis Lifeline. It's a national network of local crisis centers that provides free and confidential emotional support to people in suicidal crisis or emotional distress 24 hours a day, 7 days a week in the United States.

Call your mental health provider, doctor, or other health care provider.

Reach out to a loved one, close friend, trusted peer, or coworker.

Contact someone from your faith community.

Having unexplained aches and pains.

Feeling helpless or hopeless.

Smoking, drinking, or using drugs more than usual.

Feeling unusually confused, forgetful, on edge, angry, upset, worried, or scared.

Yelling or fighting with family and friends.

Experiencing severe mood swings that cause problems in relationships.

Having persistent thoughts and memories, you cannot get out of your head.

Hearing voices or believing things that are not true.

Thinking of harming yourself or others.

Inability to perform daily tasks like taking care of your children or getting to work or school.

If you have thoughts, fantasies, or mental images about hurting yourself or have suicidal thoughts, get help right away by taking one of these actions:

Call 911 for emergencies or your local emergency number immediately.

Call a suicide hotline number. In the US, call the National Suicide Prevention Lifeline at 1-800-273-TALK (1-800-273-8255) any time of day.

Call 988, the Suicide and Crisis Lifeline. It's a national network of local crisis centers that provides free and confidential emotional support to people in suicidal crisis or emotional distress 24 hours a day, 7 days a week in the United States.

Call your mental health provider, doctor, or other health care provider.

Reach out to a loved one, close friend, trusted peer, or coworker.

Contact someone from your faith community.

I encourage you to take an honest look at how you are doing and not minimize or gloss over signs or symptoms that may indicate a need for something to be different—whether that's better self-care, getting professional help, or something in between.

The mental health of people around the world has become of great concern. Hundreds of millions of people are suffering and struggling with some form of mental health disorder. This means that the medical and mental health communities have not done a very good job of addressing and treating the ever-growing mental health situation.

The trouble with mental health treatment today is that it tends to address symptoms but does not get to the root cause. Medication alone does not cure mental health conditions, but it can give us the ability to tend to them. With support and tools, like the ones in this book, people can choose to change their thoughts and beliefs that contributed to their condition in the first place.

Depression and Anxiety

The root cause of depression may very well have its origins in the way we learned to express or not express ourselves.

Depression is a lack of expression, and when a life event or trauma happens, subconsciously we go back to our automatic way of protecting ourselves, which may be to shut down, withdraw, and feel depressed.

Similar to depression, which is often experienced by people with anxiety, the root cause of anxiety may have its origins in the way we were raised not to show or express our feelings, especially feelings of fear.

Eating Disorders

The root cause of eating disorders is how an individual thinks and feels about themselves or a situation. Food can be used for comfort, to stuff down emotions, or to soothe them. Food can also be denied because of a distorted body image. In our formative years, we all had experiences with food—likes and dislikes—and in many households, there were power struggles over food, bonding over food, and restrictions of food. Children and teens may develop eating disorders because of comments from others about their bodies or the quantity of food they consume.

Alcohol Abuse

The root cause of alcohol abuse and most addictions stems from not having healthier coping methods. Alcohol is commonly used to self-soothe, numb emotions, and forget about problems. This goes back to how so many of us were raised—to not deal with our emotions and problems in healthy and effective ways.

Addictions

Millions of people around the world use substances to function, to get going, to calm down, and to get to sleep. We have become a society of people who self-medicate to get through life with caffeine, nicotine, alcohol, and legal and illegal drugs.

Addictions aren't limited to substances. Binge watching shows or videos, scrolling social media, overeating, gambling, and shopping are examples of avoidance behaviors that can become addictive. They are effective distractions from thinking about problems, fears, or stressors and can give us temporary relief and a false sense of feeling good.

Addictions Provide Temporary Relief

Addictions allow us to cope by temporarily numbing out or checking out emotionally—to keep overwhelming emotions of anger, resentment, sadness, grief, and other painful feelings from surfacing. Temporary relief reinforces the need to engage in addictions to feel better—and often leaves people feeling worse about themselves.

As with most addictions, the relief does not last long, and it becomes necessary to increase the behavior or substance use to get the same benefit.

Identifying as an Addict

"I am an alcoholic." "I am a binge eater." "I am a___ (fill in the blank)." Each time we identify as an addict, we tell ourselves this is who we are. It's like an affirmation that you believe because of your experience.

One of the first steps to eliminating addictive behavior is to acknowledge the behavior as a problem. The behavior is the problem; you are not the problem. And you have a behavior that needs to be addressed.

It would be more accurate to say, "I have a problem with alcohol." Or "I have a problem with the quantity of food I eat." With the specific behavior accurately defined, you can seek help, support, and solutions, which should include the factors that started you down the path of using addictive behaviors or substances to cope.

Addictions Are Symptoms

Life can be difficult, and without the ability to cope, escaping can be the next best thing. Situations like a strained relationship, a stressful job, financial difficulty, a health challenge, or other problems we don't want to face are frequently avoided by using substances or behaviors.

I have worked with hundreds of people who struggle with addictions, especially with alcohol, and I tell them, "You don't have a drinking problem; You have a need to escape or to suppress how you feel."

Addictions are symptoms of a greater problem. A person can give up drinking, and it will not solve the underlying source of why they started drinking in the first place.

Addictions are symptoms of a greater problem. A person can give up drinking, and it will not solve the underlying source of why they started drinking in the first place.

Decreasing or eliminating any addictive substance or activity is important, and there are programs to help with that. Still, if your goal is solely to stop a behavior because you believe the behavior is the problem, and not address the source of it, you will most likely struggle to overcome your addiction, or you will replace it with another addiction.

To get beyond addictions and dependencies, we must address the core problem of living in survival mode and lacking the ability to be our true, confident, and capable selves. It's vital to replace the generational programming that has kept us feeling disempowered and separated from ourselves and others, especially when it manifests in addictive behaviors.

Coping with Life's Challenges

How we cope with life's challenges is an indicator of how well we manage our thoughts and feelings about ourselves and our abilities to navigate life's ups and downs.

Addictive behaviors or substances are used as a way of coping with a situation we would rather avoid. A person could say it's because:

I don't know how to deal with my situation.
I don't want to feel the pain.
I don't know how to cope with the loss or disappointment.

Staying Stuck or Worse

Addictions over time create new challenges. A gambler may rack up debt they cannot pay back, an alcoholic may get a DUI and have their driver's license revoked, and a binge watcher may stay up late—sacrificing their sleep, health, and ability to focus. These examples also have consequences that negatively affect relationships with family and friends, the ability to parent children and perform at work.

If we don't address the root cause of why we do what we do to cope, we will miss out on the opportunity to acquire effective coping skills, feel better about ourselves, and become more resilient. When we look at how we came to function the way we do, we can make new choices. Otherwise, we will remain stuck in our disempowering ways of living and managing our lives or worse.

Chapter 10

Communication and Relationships

The moment we are born, people communicate with us verbally and nonverbally. As we grow up, we learn to adapt to the style of parenting we were raised with and to the deficits of our parents and caregivers.

As young children, we are often socialized to "be agreeable," so it's not surprising that we have a hard time saying no, sharing a different point of view, or asking for what we want. It's not uncommon for two people to get together and neither has an opinion nor wants to make a decision.

Speaking up in childhood might have come with consequences. As a child, you may have learned, "I better not speak up, or I'll get in trouble." Then as an adult, you tell yourself, "I better not say anything, or it will create a conflict."

Felicia, a woman in her fifties, said, "I hold back because if I ask for what I want, I might be seen as pushy or demanding."

Kim is in her early sixties and learned not to ask, saying, "I don't want to have to ask for anything. If I can't do something myself, I just do without it."

How we communicate or don't communicate can be a form of self-protection to keep us from feeling judged, criticized, or being made to feel bad. It can also be a way of caring for others, as in this example:

Leslie, a woman in her forties, struggles with caring for herself and suffers from health challenges. She described her relationships, saying, "I'm the rock for everyone else and not for me."

Messages about Communication

Don't speak to me in that tone of voice.
Don't talk about what goes on at our home.
Don't tell.
Don't rock the boat.
Stop asking so many questions.
Mind your own business.

Messages like these from childhood can interfere with communication between adults—causing them to hold on to secrets or not seek help or support because they believe it's not okay to ask questions, talk about problems, express themselves, or disagree.

Donna, a woman in her forties, said this about her childhood: "I didn't know what things meant, and I didn't feel like I could ask. So, I filled in the gaps the best I could. Sometimes it worked, and sometimes I got in trouble for not knowing."

Kent, a fifty-six-year-old man, told me how, during his teenage years, his parents accused him of being angry and defensive when he tried to get them to understand his position or opinion. He said, "I felt like they didn't want to hear what I had to say."

What messages do you recall about communication from your childhood?

Speaking Up

Speaking up can be challenging if you were brought up with messages like, "Children are to be seen and not heard." "Don't rock the boat." "Keep your thoughts to yourself." Or "Mind your own business."

Believing that you "have to" or "should" do what you are told or what is expected of you creates a pattern of living that doesn't allow you to consider that you have a choice or a voice. A choice to say, "I don't want to." "No, I'm not doing that." Or "I have another idea."

Ingrained messages and beliefs can interfere with speaking up about claiming your right to live a different way—a way that honors you as a human being with wants, needs, and desires.

In what ways have messages about communication kept you from speaking up?

The Challenges of Getting Along

When people don't listen, agree, or share the same opinion, strong emotions may surface. Frustration, anger, resentment, and rage give us a clue to how strong our desire is to be heard, understood, acknowledged, and accepted.

It can feel risky to voice our opinions. And when we don't trust others, it's normal to hold back as a way of protecting ourselves from judgment, conflict, rejection, disappointment, and getting hurt.

As a society, we have not done a very good job handling conflict, differences, and competing needs, which contributes to feeling separate and alone. Instead, we learned to adapt, accommodate, and defer to others to get along, belong, and survive.

Anger: The Emotion People Don't Know How to Deal With

Part of the reason some adults don't navigate the adult world well is due to expressed or unexpressed emotions, especially anger. Anger can be scary, and most people don't know what to do with an angry child, adult family member, friend, neighbor, boss, or coworker.

Anger is an emotion felt by everyone, although most of us got the message that anger was either not okay or that anger was acceptable for boys or men to express but not for girls or women. Anger is a secondary emotion, meaning that anger masks other feelings, such as frustration, hurt, fear, shame, loss, embarrassment, sadness, depression, loneliness, revengefulness, and timidness. Feeling and expressing anger during periods of conflict is less vulnerable than feeling and talking about the more painful feelings under the anger.

Hurt People Hurt People

Children who are abused, threatened, or neglected and are not allowed to speak up or express their hurts and disappointments may lash out at their peers or siblings or bully others who are weaker. They hurt others because they don't have a healthy outlet for their feelings or someone they trust to talk to about how bad they feel. Hurt children can grow up to become adults who continue to hurt others until they suffer enough consequences or choose to develop healthier ways of interacting.

Communication Responses

The way we respond to others can foster communication or sever it. When a question is met with defensiveness, the person asking may feel attacked. When a question is met with an apology when one is not called for, the person responding can come across as having done something wrong. When someone answers a question without emotion but a simple yes or no, they can appear disengaged. When someone answers a question with a lie, saying, "I didn't do it," they aren't being truthful. And when a person answers a question with anger, the message might sound blaming.

Each of these responses creates distance, cuts off conversation, creates arguments and hurt feelings, and can feel confusing. This is what happens when we don't feel worthy, deserving, and secure in who we are to express ourselves or to listen to understand and thoughtfully reply.

The Effects of Parenting on Communication and Relationships

How we communicate and the quality of our relationships are related to the way we were parented. Back in the 1800s, sons were the "property" of their fathers until they turned twenty-one, and they were required to either work for their fathers on the farm or for a neighboring farmer. Girls stayed home and worked alongside their mothers learning to be housewives, or they could work for neighbors and give their fathers most or all of their earnings. Parents were allowed to (and usually did) keep much control over their children in years past.

Fast forward to the 1910s, when parents were encouraged to refrain from touching their babies as much as possible, as it was believed that too much love and affection had a negative effect on a child's resilience.

It's not surprising that exerting a high level of parental control and denying touch to babies would produce generations of children who would have deficits in the adult world—especially communicating and interacting with others. There have been many styles of parenting over the years, and authoritarian parenting continues to be the most common one used today.

Authoritarian Parenting

An authoritarian parent focuses more on obedience, discipline, and control rather than nurturing and connecting with their child. The parents make rules and set high expectations but lack warmth and support. Authoritarian parents tend to "rule with an iron fist." They are often described as cold, strict, critical, punitive, and demanding. They are not interested in responses or two-way communication with their children. This rigid parenting style uses stern discipline, often justified as "tough love." In an attempt to be in total control, authoritarian parents often talk to their children without wanting input or feedback.

Children of authoritarian parenting are apt to exhibit low self-esteem, poor social skills and academic competence, poor decision making, and low creativity. They also tend to have problems such as depression, emotional suppression, behavioral issues, and fear of failure. It is only recently that we have begun to become aware of the emotional needs of children, as more and more children are exhibiting anxiety and having difficulty coping with everyday life. Parenting by control has not worked to produce children who are happy, feel good about themselves, and grow up to become adults who are confident, happy, resilient, and expressive.

Adapting to Family Members

In many families, the primary focus is on the individual with the most power. It could be the one who earns the most money, the one who has a physical condition, or the one who makes the most noise. Children who grow up in families where a significant amount of attention is on a needy parent or sibling can feel left out or neglected and that they and their needs don't matter.

Adults who grew up in families like these tend to fall into the same familiar patterns from childhood by taking a back seat to others whose needs are greater than theirs.

Respecting Ourselves and Others

How can we have respect for ourselves and others when we have been conditioned to ignore our needs, body signals, feelings, and ourselves? Adults who grew up not honoring their feelings and needs learned to shut down, act out, or numb their feelings.

We are seeing the effects of what I call "self-betrayal." Self-betrayal is when a person acts out of obligation or does what they were conditioned to do because they don't want to hurt or offend someone or because they don't want to risk saying no or getting someone upset with them.

Each time we say yes to someone else and no to our own needs, we are betraying ourselves.

Each time we say yes to someone else and no to our own needs, we are betraying ourselves.

The effects of disrespecting ourselves and our needs have negative consequences for everyone. Anger, resentment, rebelliousness, and self-harm are common in people who lack self-respect. Addictive behaviors and avoidance become how we relate to ourselves and others, creating distance in relationships and further distancing from our need to express ourselves in healthy ways.

Codependency

Codependency is a psychological concept that refers to people who feel extreme amounts of dependence on certain loved ones in their lives and who feel responsible for the feelings and actions of those loved ones.

Codependent traits, like the following, can be traced back to early childhood conditioning.

Codependent people:

Tend to love people they can pity and rescue.
Feel responsible for the actions of others.
Do more than their share in the relationship to keep the peace.
Are afraid of being abandoned or alone.
Feel responsible for their partner's happiness.
Need approval from others to gain their own self-worth.
Have difficulty making decisions and often doubt themselves.
Are reluctant to trust others.
Base their moods on the thoughts and feelings of those around them.

Codependency has been recognized as a relationship dynamic that affects people with all kinds of childhood trauma, not just the children or spouses of alcoholics or substance abusers, leading them to feel anxious or insecure about relationships.

It's common for adults who have been "parentified" as children to be more likely to be codependent. Parentification refers to "the reversal of the parent-child role," or when a child serves in a parental or caretaking role toward their own parent. This is usually due to the parent not having had their own developmental needs met while they were growing up. Since codependent children grow up not having their developmental needs met either, this can create a cycle of codependency passed down from generation to generation.

Given our generational conditioning, most of us could be labeled codependent.

People with codependent traits are often perfectionistic and self-critical; fixing or rescuing others makes them feel needed. They focus so much on pleasing others that they neglect their own wants and needs. They generally have low self-esteem, find it hard to set boundaries and be assertive, and struggle with asking for help when they need it. Eventually, the codependent becomes frustrated, exhausted, and burned out, leading to increased conflicts and dissatisfaction with the relationship.

Given our generational conditioning, most of us could be labeled codependent.

What codependent traits do you most identify with?

How does codependency show up in your relationships?

In what ways were you conditioned to take on codependent ways of thinking, feeling, and acting?

Raised to Be Overly Independent

The opposite of codependent is overly independent. Children raised to become overly independent tend to have a belief that they must do everything on their own and not ask for help. Collectively, over the last several decades, adults have become overly independent and separate from each other to the extent that a lack of connection is creating measurable problems of loneliness, insufficient family support, and a decrease in caring for one another.

It used to be that people knew their neighbors and others in their communities and looked out for each other. Now, it has become common to look the other way and stay to ourselves even though this goes against our innate nature to belong.

Chapter 11

Divorce and Loyalty Conflicts

Divorce and loyalty conflicts go hand in hand, although loyalty conflicts can be found anywhere people connect. Adapting to divorce or the wants, demands, or threats of a parent, partner, boss, coworker, sibling, or friend can cause us to feel fearful, angry and resentful, or numb. Our desire to belong is so strong that as children and as adults, we often go along with being loyal even when it conflicts with what we want, how we want to act, or the way we would like to be treated.

Early childhood experiences that include loyalty conflicts are often overlooked when trying to figure out how to get along with others and have a sense of belonging. Also, loyalty conflicts and divorce can negatively impact our perception and belief about what a healthy relationship looks like.

If you are a child of divorce, divorced, or are with someone who has experienced divorce, this chapter will help you understand more about yourself and your partner.

Divorce

Almost fifty percent of all marriages in the United States will end in divorce or separation. Globally, in the nearly four decades between 1970 and 2008, the divorce rate more than doubled, from 2.6 divorces for every 1,000 married people to 5.5.

While two adults may not always agree on getting divorced, it's the adults, not the children, who decide. And adults are generally the ones who determine how their children will split their time between their parents' homes.

Divorce can have adverse effects on children. These include signs of distress such as acting out, mental or emotional instability, regressive behavior, and a decline in academics. Insecurity and anxiety are common as many children feel neglected, depressed, or distracted by the loss of their family as they have known it. Some children blame themselves for their parents' divorce, while others may feel abandoned.

Some of the long-term effects on adults from divorced homes are that they are more likely to get divorced. That is, if they choose to marry. Also, adults from divorced homes may be less willing to enter a long-term, committed relationship out of fear of their relationship not lasting.

Adjusting to Divorce

If your parents divorced when you were a child or you experienced divorce as an adult, you might identify with some of the challenges above. Additionally, adults may have difficulty balancing their needs and the needs of their children while being a single parent. Children can be confused about their roles after a divorce. They are often expected to be more like an adult, taking on more responsibility, while still being a child.

Bringing new people into a child's life through dating and remarriage has its challenges too. It's a lot of change for a child who feels powerless over the choices their divorced parents make that impact them. And having a stepparent creates new dynamics between the adults and children, especially when the stepparent has children, creating a blended family.

When Divorce Is the Right Decision

Divorce can be a devastating experience for the adults who are splitting and for their children. But it can be an empowering and sometimes even a life-saving choice when the alternative of staying in the marriage is detrimental. Some marriages are abusive, posing risks to the emotional and physical well-being and even the survival of adults and children. It can be an act of love for yourself and your children (if you have any) to leave such a marriage.

Loyalties and Loyalty Conflicts During Childhood

I saw firsthand the effects of loyalty conflicts in children when I was working with high-conflict divorce families. It was common for them to come from homes with situations or allegations of domestic violence, child abuse, and substance abuse. This often resulted in the court appointment of a child custody evaluation to sort out the truth and then recommend what was in the children's best interest.

The concept of loyalty conflicts doesn't just happen in high-conflict families or divorced families. Loyalty conflicts also happen in two-parent families where there are tensions between parents or different parenting styles, and they can happen in friendship circles and workplaces. I believe loyalty conflicts happen more often than we are aware of, in both childhood and adulthood.

Loyalty Conflicts from a Child's Perspective

Loyalty conflicts often occur in high-conflict families and the following is from my work with children who had highly conflictual parents.

When a child is raised by high-conflict parents, it's common for the child to align with one parent, creating a loyalty conflict that can mildly to severely affect the ability of the child to have a positive relationship with the other parent. The child sides with one parent as a way of coping with the conflict between their parents.

A child involved in a loyalty conflict learns to compartmentalize their feelings and will often act differently—by ignoring or being rude or disrespectful to the other parent when in the presence of both parents when they usually are not that way. They may feel uncomfortable showing affection to one or both parents in front of the other parent.

It's common for children with loyalty conflicts to tell one or both parents what they think they want to hear, which means they learn to create half-truths, lie, make up stories, minimize or exaggerate, and hide the truth. This can lead to the child feeling guilt and shame, having difficulties with friendships, and not being honest with themselves.

The Emotional Pain of Loyalty Conflicts

When children become angry and disrespectful, it leads to consequences at home and school. This includes having something of value taken away, an item or something they were looking forward to, time-outs, and in some cases, physical punishment by an angry or frustrated parent. More importantly, the core feelings of loss, hurt, sadness, and disappointment don't get addressed, resulting in an accumulation of stored emotions that inevitably leak out as anger, irritability, somatic symptoms, or turn into depression. Emotional pain can also be covered up by being accommodating or compliant or avoided by addictive behaviors or substances.

As a way of coping, a child may align with one parent and take on that parent's anger and hate of the other parent as a way of dealing or not dealing with their pain. This way, they don't have to feel the hurt, pain, sadness, and loss of their family and the relationship with the other parent. These children grow up with a storehouse of emotions they have no outlet for until their suppressed emotions surface in adulthood.

The Effects of Loyalty Conflicts on Decision Making and Trust

Children with loyalty conflicts tend to have difficulty making decisions. They may become compliant and go along with what others are doing, or they may become defiant or rebellious or make poor decisions without thinking through the outcome and consequences of their decisions.

A child in a loyalty conflict between their parents may have difficulty trusting either parent. Over time they often come to resent the parent they were loyal to. This usually happens in adulthood when they gain some awareness about the position they were put in or when they choose to develop a closer connection with the non-aligned parent.

Overt and Covert Messages about Being Loyal

While the words may or may not be spoken out loud, the messages a child receives while in a loyalty conflict from the aligned parent can sound or feel like these, "If you don't do as I say, there will be a price to pay." "If you don't do what I want you to do, there will be a consequence." "I won't support you or take you where you want to go or buy you that thing you want if you don't do what I tell you."

One of the worst messages a child can hear is, "If you agree with your mother or father, I can't have you in my life." or "If you take your mom's or dad's side, I will disown you."

Loyalty Conflict Patterns

Two patterns often develop from loyalty conflicts in childhood. The first is suppressing thoughts and feelings that conflict with the aligned parent. The child begins to betray themself by doing what someone else wants them to do rather than what they want to do or believe is right for them. They give up a piece of themself to please someone else so they will be taken care of, accepted, or loved. There often is a strong need to keep the peace at any cost. So, they give up having an individual identity, and with that, they sacrifice their values, needs, wants, and desires.

The second common pattern is that children who grow up with loyalty conflicts develop adaptive patterns that get recreated in adulthood with others. They may subconsciously align with or against friends, coworkers, or other family members because this is a safe and familiar way of relating to others.

Chapter 12

Enemies and Violence

The model of war and increased violence worldwide has caused people to fear each other and refrain from connecting with those who are different from them or share different views and values. In today's world, people who are different from us or think differently are often viewed as wrong and untrustworthy. There is a lack of willingness to share thoughts and ideas that could lead to mutual or compromised decisions. This fixed view has resulted in severed relationships and sometimes violence. Historically, violence has been a way of controlling others, and as you will see, it's imbedded in our culture, language, and media.

Messages about Enemies and People Who Are Different from Us

If they aren't one of us, we can't trust them.

They are our enemies.

Stick with your own kind.

When I was growing up, I was told that Germans, Russians, and people in gangs were dangerous. In today's divided society, we have been taught that people who think, believe, and act differently from us are not to be trusted and are enemies.

To generalize that *all* people from a geographical part of the world are dangerous has caused us as adults to hate countries and groups of people who are different from us when only a small segment of them are dishonest, dangerous, have caused, or continue to cause harm. The same has been said about different ethnicities, cultures, religions, political groups, and governments. It's no wonder we lack respect for ourselves and others, because we must distance ourselves from those who are a perceived threat.

What messages did you grow up with about people who are different from you?

What effect have these messages had on you and your relationship with others?

The Model of War and Violent Language

When I think of war, I think of damage, destruction, injuries, and casualties. War has been a messy model. Being at war is a high price to pay to gain a result. Many of us are at war with ourselves, believing we must fight an urge, battle our weight, or attack an illness.

Our language is embedded with words of force. We are accustomed to sayings like:

Shoot me an email.

Give it a shot.

You must fight for what you want.

I'm just killing time.

The traffic was murder.

I'm going to hit the road.

We've also had "fighting" type language in slogans to address societal problems:

The war on drugs.

The war on cancer.

We must fight poverty.

Violence in the World

The world has not been a safe place for a really long time, and over the last couple of decades, going about our daily lives has felt dangerous.

If we look at history since the 1900s, it began with World War I in 1914, and after four years, more than 16 million soldiers and civilians were killed. Then in September of 1939, Hitler's invasion of Poland marked the beginning of World War II. Over the next six years, the conflict took more lives (an estimated 70-85 million military and civilian deaths) and destroyed more land and property around the globe than any previous war. Also during that time was the Holocaust from 1939 to 1941, resulting in the systematic extermination of six million Jews, Gypsies, homosexuals, and other people by Nazi Germany.

While the destruction of these events and other wars occurred abroad, the terrorist attacks of 9/11 brought terrifying violence to the United States. On the day of September 11, 2001, four airplanes were hijacked, carrying out suicide attacks against targets in the United States. Two planes were flown into the twin towers of the World Trade Center in New York City, a third plane hit the Pentagon in Arlington, Virginia, just outside Washington, DC, and the fourth plane crashed in a field in Shanksville, Pennsylvania. During the attacks, 2,977 people were killed, and over 6,000 others were injured.

Violence in Schools

School shootings are not new and are of great concern to parents and students. The earliest known United States shooting to happen on school property was the Pontiac's Rebellion school massacre on July 26, 1764, where four Lenape American Indians entered the schoolhouse near present-day Greencastle, Pennsylvania, and shot and killed the schoolmaster and nine or ten children.

There were twelve reported school shootings in the 1800s. During the 1900s, there were just under 100 school shootings, including (at that time) the nation's deadliest school shooting on April 20, 1999, in Littleton, Colorado, where fourteen students (including the shooters) and one teacher were killed and twenty-seven others wounded at Columbine High School. Two students had plotted for a year to kill at least 500 and blow up their school. At the end of their hour-long rampage, they turned their guns on themselves (K12 Academics, n.d.).

Since 1999, there have been a staggering number of school shootings with significantly higher deaths and injuries, causing grief and loss in communities and fear in parents and children about the safety of attending school.

Violence and Children

There has been an increase in both school shootings and mass shootings. Is it safe to go to school? Is it safe to go shopping, to a concert, or to a sporting event?

Many people have gone from "home isn't safe" to "the world doesn't feel safe."

What causes someone to carry out hideous acts of violence? Early childhood programming of disempowering messages combined with adverse childhood experiences can produce individuals who become so mentally and emotionally disturbed that they act out the magnitude of their pain on others.

Generally, these individuals feel like they don't belong, they don't feel safe, and they don't feel loved or cared about. Contributing factors that lead to perpetrating violence on others come from generations of learned behavior from childhood abuse and desensitization to violence from watching or experiencing abuse. More recently, electronics have given adults and children easy access to viewing violence in movies, video games, television, and the news.

According to The American Academy of Child and Adolescent Psychiatry (AACAP 2017), hundreds of studies on the effects of TV violence on children and teenagers have found that children may:

Become "immune" or numb to the horror of violence
Begin to accept violence as a way to solve problems
Imitate the violence they observe on television
Identify with certain characters, victims, and/or victimizers

Extensive viewing of television violence by children causes greater aggressiveness. Sometimes, watching a single violent program can increase aggressiveness. Children who view shows in which violence is very realistic, frequently repeated, or unpunished are more likely to imitate what they see. Children with emotional, behavioral, learning, or impulse control problems may be more easily influenced by TV violence. The impact of TV violence may show immediately in a child's behavior or may surface years later. Also, young people can be affected even when their home life shows no tendency toward violence.

What comes to your mind when you think about the amount of violence we are exposed to regularly?

Distress

Children are in distress; adults are in distress, and it seems to be getting worse. The way we have been addressing violence and abuse is not working. In many parts of the world, systems are in place to bring justice to victims and punish or incarcerate those found guilty. Unfortunately, most acts of violence and abuse don't get reported, and when they do, it can be a long and drawn-out emotional process to go through a court or government system.

Getting to the root cause of the problem of abuse and violence entails finding ways to prevent individuals from harming themselves and others. When enough people truly value themselves and others, I believe we will see media that models constructive, nonviolent ways to solve problems.

The serious problems we face today are primarily due to generations of:

Disempowering early childhood messages
Adverse experiences in childhood and adulthood
Abuse, fighting, and killing to solve problems
Punishment rather than teaching, modeling, and rehabilitation

By becoming aware of what is causing and keeping so many people in distress, we can take effective steps to prevent these patterns from continuing. There is evidence of hope, and we all have a role to play! Individuals are capable of making lasting positive changes, and that includes you.

Communities come together when natural disasters occur. America came together after the 9/11 attacks, and the world came together at the beginning of the 2020 pandemic. We are capable of working together, but often it does not last long because we lose sight of helping each other and go back to our familiar individualistic coping patterns and ways of living.

What tends to work is the opposite of being at war. It may seem strange to think that being in harmony is more effective, but it is. When we are in harmony with an illness, an addiction, or another person, we are not fighting. This allows us the opportunity to find new solutions, new ways of coping, and new ways of relating to one another.

When we acknowledge what is going on, it has less power over us. And by listening to our body's message or looking at the situation objectively, we can grow from it, deal with it, course correct, find a new way, a new treatment, or choose to forgive. Harmony allows us to get along, coexist, cocreate, support each other, and heal.

Chapter 13

All Childhood Experiences Matter

If you think childhood experiences don't matter because children are too young to remember them, that's just not true. Life is full of adversities, and there are many a child shouldn't have to experience, such as abuse or neglect.

The good news is that adverse experiences can be countered by positive experiences at any age. Both positive and negative experiences from childhood shape us into who we become as adults. In this chapter, there are specific questions to find out what positive experiences you had during your childhood, but first, let's look at what studies have shown about traumatic experiences in childhood.

Adverse Childhood Experiences Study (ACES)

A ten-item questionnaire was developed in 1985 by Dr. Vincent Felitti to assess and measure adults for ten types of childhood trauma. Five are personal: physical abuse, verbal abuse, sexual abuse, physical neglect, and emotional neglect. Five are related to other family members: a parent who is an alcoholic, a mother who is a victim of domestic violence, a family member in jail, a family member diagnosed with a mental illness, and the disappearance of a parent through divorce, death, or abandonment.

There are, of course, many other types of childhood trauma—racism, bullying, watching a sibling being abused, losing a caregiver (grandmother, grandfather, etc.), homelessness, surviving and recovering from a severe accident, witnessing a father being abused by a mother, witnessing a grandmother abusing a father, involvement with the foster care system, involvement with the juvenile justice system, and so on.

The CDC's Adverse Childhood Experiences Study, using the ten-item questionnaire, uncovered a direct link between childhood trauma and the chronic diseases people develop as adults, as well as social and emotional problems. This includes heart disease, lung cancer, diabetes, and many autoimmune diseases, as well as depression, violence, being a victim of violence, and suicide.

The first research results were published in 1998, followed by more than seventy other publications through 2015.

They showed that:

Childhood trauma was very common, even in employed, white middle-class, college-educated people with great health insurance.

The more types of traumas experienced increased the risk of health, social and emotional problems.

People usually experience more than one type of trauma. Rarely is it only sexual abuse or only verbal abuse.

When children have adverse experiences, they are in a fight, flight, fright, or freeze mode. Stress and stress hormones prevent them from having the ability to focus and learn in school. Adverse experiences cause children to have difficulty trusting adults and developing healthy relationships with peers, leading them to become loners. To escape their problems and relieve their anxiety, guilt, shame, depression, and inability to focus, they may turn to easily available substances like marijuana, nicotine, alcohol, and methamphetamine—or activities like overachievement, work, overeating, or high-risk sports, to name a few.

Using drugs, overeating, or engaging in risky behavior leads to consequences as a direct result of this behavior. For example, smoking can lead to lung cancer. Overeating can lead to obesity and diabetes. Additionally, there is increasing research that shows that severe and chronic stress causes an inflammatory response that leads to disease.

Physician Gabor Maté, in his book, *The Myth of Normal: Trauma, Illness, and Healing in a Toxic Culture,* details the effects of trauma on our bodies (Maté 2022).

It has been said by Dr. Felitti, the developer of the ACES questionnaire, that adverse childhood experiences are at the root of nearly all problems of physical, mental, economic, and social health in humans, no matter where in the world those humans live.

It has been said by Dr. Felitti, the developer of the ACES questionnaire, that adverse childhood experiences are at the root of nearly all problems of physical, mental, economic, and social health in humans, no matter where in the world those humans live.

For a more in-depth look, Oprah Winfrey and trauma expert Dr. Bruce Perry approach the understanding of the effects of early childhood traumas and adversity as a way that leads to healing and the development of resiliency in their book, *What Happened to You?* (Perry, Winfrey 2021).

Child Abuse

You may not have to look too far to identify with an abused child. The definition of child abuse is when a parent or caretaker physically, emotionally, or sexually abuses, neglects, or abandons a child. Child abuse is more common than people tend to believe. There was an incident in my childhood that produced a welt on my body and would have been reportable.

Historically, child protection in America first started in colonial times. Then in 1875, the creation and growth of organized child protection through nongovernmental child protection societies came about. It wasn't until 1962 that government-sponsored Child Protective Services (CPS) began.

While child protection laws and services are in place in the United States, the system as it currently is does not adequately protect children. Child abuse remains excessively high, while social workers are expected to handle extremely large caseloads, often leading to burnout or leaving their jobs.

Positive Childhood Experiences

In 2019, a team of researchers found an association between positive childhood experiences and adult mental and relationship health among adults who had experienced Adverse Childhood Experiences (ACEs), irrespective of how many ACEs they had. This means it is crucial to have positive childhood experiences, no matter how much adversity you have in your life. If you have a lot of adversity and a lot of positive childhood experiences, you are less likely to suffer the consequences of ACEs. However, if you have no positive childhood experiences and few ACEs, the consequences of the ACEs are more likely to appear.

To find out what positive childhood experiences you have had, answer the following questions. How much or how often during your childhood did you:

Feel able to talk to your family about your feelings?

Feel your family stood by you during difficult times?

Enjoy participating in community traditions?

Feel a sense of belonging in high school?

Feel supported by friends?

Have at least two nonparent adults who took a genuine interest in you?

Feel safe and protected by an adult in your home? (*JAMA Pediatrics* 2019)

Negative and Positive Experiences

We have all experienced situations during our lifetime that have colored our lives, causing us to focus on what's gone wrong. It's like living in murky water.

At any age, we can counter the "adversities of life" with positive experiences to balance the negative ones. When we temporarily stop focusing on the bad stuff and dilute it with positive experiences, we interrupt the pattern of negativity and instill new connections in our brains. Over time, doing things we enjoy and having more positive experiences will "dilute the murky water" and bring a greater sense of peace, calm, and wellness.

Because of the nature of the world we live in, there will be challenges to deal with, and you can give them the attention they need without swimming in negativity by adding things to your life that bring you joy and happiness.

Part 3

Becoming Your True Self

Chapter 14

You Have the Power

In part 1 and part 2 you discovered an enormous amount of information about the disempowering messages and experiences you grew up with and now we are going to begin to replace the generational conditioning you received so that you can have positive, satisfying, rewarding experiences—and feel good about being your true self.

What If the Worst Is behind You?

What happened has happened. Your early childhood programming and experiences happened. It was long ago, and you are not that same child anymore. You're all grown up, and you have the power to change the patterns from the past and the limited thinking that got created. I can tell you that when you live from your empowered, grown-up self—not your subconscious child self—your life will get better in ways you cannot even imagine.

Given your history, the history of your parents, and the generations before them, your life could not have happened any differently. Take a deep breath and know that the worst *is* behind you. From your self-reflection of the childhood messages and experiences you had, you now have the knowledge and power to replace generational patterns that have been running your life. Remember, you are not that young, dependent, helpless child that didn't have a choice about your conditioning, and you have been doing the best you can.

Take a moment and acknowledge yourself for all that you have been through.

Take a moment and acknowledge yourself for all that you have been through.

I know what is possible because I have experienced it myself and have successfully guided thousands of people through the process of replacing their old conditioning so that they no longer continue to live by it—and I want that for you!

Focusing on You

It may feel awkward, foreign, or uncomfortable to focus on yourself in positive ways. It might be challenging if the messages in your subconscious say to think of others and not yourself or that it's selfish to put yourself first, as illustrated in this client story.

Ava is a woman in her early sixties who came to me to improve her health. Her doctor told her she needed to take medication for diabetes, or she would experience permanent damage to her body. Ava did not understand how she became so unhealthy and why she struggled to take care of her basic needs, including the need to take medication.

During our work together, we uncovered the feelings of guilt she had about taking care of herself because it was ingrained in her at a young age that she was not supposed to do things for herself. Once we made the connection and worked with the messages from her childhood that were getting in the way, she was more consistent with her medication and began taking better care of her overall health.

It is *essential* to think of yourself and to put yourself first!

It is *essential* to think of yourself and to put yourself first!

A significant part of the difficulties we face individually and collectively stem from being disconnected from ourselves, putting others first, and looking outside of ourselves for everything—especially approval, worth, and love.

You have the power to *stop*!

The power to stop letting your childhood conditioning and your past define you.

The power to stop blaming yourself and putting yourself down.

The power to stop neglecting yourself.

Remember, you did not create your programming, and it's not your fault. *And*, you have the power to build a stronger inner foundation, for a happier life.

Replacing Messages, Beliefs, and Patterns

You are in charge here. You get to make the rules. You get to choose what you do, and if you don't like it, you get to change your mind and do something else. You get to honor your needs and go at your own pace. With that said, my hopes are that you will approach what you choose with anticipation of an improved life or situation.

When you replace your thoughts about the messages you received in early childhood you change the programming in your brain. It's that simple. By replacing your programming, those old messages will no longer have the same power over you.

I encourage you to take some time to identify a message, belief, or pattern that you want to replace. Be as specific as you can.

Here are some examples:

I choose to no longer live by the message that it is selfish to put myself first.

I choose to no longer believe that it is bad or wrong to tend to my needs.

I choose to no longer think that my needs are not important or that I am not important.

Finish these sentences with a message, belief, or pattern you want to replace:

I choose to no longer live by the message, belief, or pattern _____.

I choose to no longer think that _____.

Letting Go

Once you choose what you no longer want to think, believe, or live by, it may bring up feelings of sadness, anger, or grief. It's common to feel the loss of what you needed or wanted and didn't get. As you say goodbye to old ways of thinking, believing, or living, know that these have been lifelong patterns, and it may take some time to shift to new ways of thinking, believing, and living. When you are ready, you will let go, change your thinking, and set yourself free from the old programming that is not serving you well today.

Chapter 15

Replacing Patterns of Thoughts

To get beyond the messages and labels put on us as children or adults, or by our own doing, we need to take a different approach to how we think, feel, act, and cope with our challenges rather than be defined by them.

When we do something in the same way over and over, it becomes a pattern of functioning. And for the most part, that is a good thing. Imagine if we had to think about every little movement to start our day, such as getting out of bed, brushing our teeth, and getting dressed. It would take a lot of time and energy. Our miraculous human brain was designed to be efficient. That means repeating something becomes a pattern, something we don't have to think about.

The patterns we observed in childhood repeat themselves. The experiences we had became our patterns, and they feel familiar. And the familiar—whether good or bad—feels comfortable.

So comfortable that on some level we often prefer the familiar over the unknown.

We learned to function, cope, and adapt to the circumstances from our formative years out of the need to survive. In part 2, you discovered the messages that created your survival patterns. This valuable information will help you decide what you want to do differently.

Our thoughts are powerful, and what we think about and focus on is what we expect, look for, and experience. Most of this takes place subconsciously, based on childhood programming we did not choose.

We cannot expect a better outcome if we automatically have the same thoughts, feelings, and emotions, and the same ways of acting. Therefore, we must intentionally replace patterns that don't serve us well.

We cannot expect a better outcome if we automatically have the same thoughts, feelings, and emotions, and the same ways of acting. Therefore, we must intentionally replace patterns that don't serve us well.

Patterns of Thoughts
Neural pathways in our brain are created by thoughts and associations we make from events and outcomes, and they

become more solid with repetition. In other words, as we think the same thoughts repeatedly, they become ingrained in our brain.

Since our thoughts determine how we feel, what we do, and the meaning we make from our experiences—it is essential to become aware of our thought patterns and shift those that are not working for us.

Patterns of thought are where most of our positive changes will come from. Because of our need to survive, our default mode has been to focus on problems. We anticipate problems and are on the lookout for them. That is our survival brain in action. Problem-focused thinking produces stress, anxiety, worrying, and complaining, which keeps us from thinking about possible solutions. Problem-focused thinking alone does not work, and it is not good for our health and well-being.

If we are ever going to solve our problems or improve a situation, we must become solution focused.

If we are ever going to solve our problems or improve a situation, we must become solution focused.

Learning New Ways of Thinking

The way to get the most out of this chapter is to take your time reading and considering how you might use one or more solution-focused ways of thinking. You don't need to use them all! Each of the different solution-focused ways of thinking has questions or examples. Choose one or two of them to practice using.

As with anything unfamiliar, thinking in new ways may seem like a foreign language, and it's common to feel awkward. It's also normal to fear how others will react to your new ways of thinking as you express yourself differently. Fear may also arise when you come up against limiting beliefs you have about what is possible. It's all normal. Remember that it's your survival thinking and programming that is getting in the way of you trusting yourself with new ways of thinking.

As you practice new ways of thinking, go at your own pace. You must feel *comfortable enough* that you can handle the changes. Otherwise, you will revert to old survival patterns. Each time you think in solution-focused ways, you are building new neural pathways in your brain, and eventually, thinking about good, possible, and positive outcomes will become your new automatic way of thinking.

Whether a problem is physical, emotional, personal, financial, or has to do with a relationship, it is helpful to think about the problem as temporary, not permanent.

Whether a problem is physical, emotional, personal, financial, or has to do with a relationship, it is helpful to think about the problem as temporary, not permanent.

Possibility Thinking

One of the most powerful ways to approach a problem is with possibility thinking. When you think about what is possible, it puts you in the mindset to receive new information, options, and new perspectives.

Here's an example of a problem-focused way of thinking: There is too much to do, and I have to do it all myself.

This problem-focused thinking tends to produce anxiety and a high level of stress that may lead to obsessive thoughts and sleepless nights.

Here's an example of a solution-focused way of thinking: I can gather the information and delegate, hire, or have someone else do what needs to be done.

This solution-focused thinking creates healthy boundaries and distributes responsibility.

Think about a situation, then use these possibility thinking questions for solution-focused thinking:

What else is possible?
What can I do differently?
Is there another way to do this?
Is there an easier way to do this?
Who can help me?

Curiosity Thinking

Do you remember being a curious kid? We were born curious. It's how we learned and discovered new things. Without curiosity, we might not inquire about how things work or want to know what something is.

Unfortunately, most of us lost our curiosity thinking when we went to school and were expected to listen to what was being taught. Or we might have been told to stop asking so many questions.

Adults can cultivate a curiosity mindset—wondering what will happen combined with a desire to figure something out or to know or learn something new.

Curiosity thinking is the opposite of assuming you know something or how something will turn out. It's having an open mind to seek and take in new information and ask questions.

Here are some curiosity-thinking questions to ask yourself.

I wonder:

What's going to happen today?
Who will I meet?
What will I hear?
What will I see?
What will I read?
What will I create?

As you become more curious, expect new thoughts and ideas to come to you.

Clarity

To have clarity is one of the most wonderful things you can experience! It is that feeling when you know what direction to take or what decision to make.

It's easy to get confused by all the information we have access to and what others tell us to do. Clarity gives you direction and provides a feeling of knowing you are making a wise decision or the right decision for yourself, your health, or anything else. Clarity thinking is most effective when you pose a question to yourself and then tune in to how you feel as you think about your options.

Ask yourself clarity thinking questions like these:

What is the next best thing for me to do?
What am I inspired to do?
Do I really want to _____?
Is it better to buy _____ or _____?
Is now the time to _____, or is it best to wait?
Is what is being recommended the best for me and this situation?

When you do not know what to do about a situation or what decision to make, check in with yourself to get clarity. The more you practice asking yourself clarifying questions, the better you will get at tuning into your inner knowing.

In addition to possibility thinking, curiosity thinking, and thinking that produces clarity, here are several more ways to change your thought patterns. They include:

Opposite Thinking
Forward Thinking
Positive "What If" Thinking

Each of these, on its own, will broaden your thinking and replace the survival thinking that keeps you repeating old patterns of feelings and actions. By thinking differently, you will begin to reprogram your brain, and over time it will become automatic to think more broadly.

Opposite Thinking

Since our brains are wired to look for what is wrong or what is dangerous for survival, we have a negativity bias to overcome. Negative thoughts about how others treat you or how you treat yourself may include judgment, criticism, or disrespect. None of these thoughts have to do with you being in immediate danger!

The pattern of negative thinking and negative conclusions about yourself can be replaced with opposite thinking. When you notice negative thoughts about yourself or others, try replacing them with their opposite.

Here are some examples to experiment with.

Replace thoughts of judgment or being judged with thoughts of approval or acceptance: They approve of me. They approve of my work. I am accepted. I approve of what I am doing. I accept myself.

Replace thoughts of criticism or being criticized with thoughts of praise or compliments: That turned out well. I enjoy receiving compliments. I look good in these clothes. I like that I am being true to myself.

Replace thoughts of disrespect or being disrespected with thoughts of respect or friendliness: Just because my boss is having a bad day does not mean I need to take it on. I can be friendly to those who are struggling. I can treat myself with kindness when I am having a tough time.

Replace negative conclusions about yourself with these opposites:

Replace worthlessness with worthiness: I am worthy.

Replace being taken for granted with appreciation: I appreciate how I help others when I choose to help them.

Replace undeserving thoughts with deserving thoughts: I am deserving. I am just as deserving as anyone else. I deserve to have my needs met and feel supported.

Here are some additional opposite ways of thinking for you to personalize:

Replace unhappy thoughts with happy thoughts.
Replace problem-focused thinking with solution-focused thinking.
Replace not expecting what you want with expecting what you want.

Forward Thinking

When negative thoughts from the past are dominant—like past failures and undesirable experiences—you can replace them with forward thinking. Rather than thinking about what has happened, think about what you would like to have happen.

Forward thinking puts your thinking in the direction of what *do* want.

Forward thinking puts your thinking in the direction of what you *do* want.

Use your imagination as you think about what you want or what you would prefer. Notice what thoughts and feelings come up as you think about what you *do* want.

Here are three prompts to get you started:

What I really want is…
What I prefer is…
What I would love is…

What did you learn about yourself? Did it feel good to focus on what you want? Did you notice any doubts or fears? The next way of thinking will enhance positive feelings of what you want and replace thoughts that are getting in the way.

Positive "What If" Thinking

It's possible to do, be, or have what you desire once you replace the early childhood programming preventing you from what you want. Positive "What If" thinking broadens your view of possibilities. It allows you to dream, imagine, and replace old ways of thinking.

Here are three examples of positive "What if" thinking.

What if people do want to hear what I have to say? What if others are happy to listen to what I have to say? What if they like my ideas? What if my ideas are valuable? What if they want to hear more? What if they want to hire me?

What if I went to the party and had a good time? What if I met someone interesting there? What if I met a new friend? What if I met someone I could date? What if I met my future partner at the party?

What if it could be easier than I thought? What if I am so ready for something better and it happens quickly? What if I could be living my new and better life today? What if I could feel happier, healthier, and genuinely good right now?

Now it is your turn. Try one of your own "What if" scenarios. What if…

Could you feel a difference with this way of thinking? Do you feel more excited, energized, or optimistic? If this way of thinking is uncomfortable, notice the thoughts that are getting in the way of thinking about positive outcomes. Remember, your current thoughts are based on the messages you grew up with, along with your life experiences. Use this way of thinking to imagine favorable possibilities, even if you don't believe they will happen or know how they will happen. The goal is to shift your thinking, and over time, as you experience positive results, it will become easier to think about and imagine what you want.

"Imagination is everything. It is the preview of life's coming attractions." Albert Einstein

---

"Imagination is everything. It is the preview of life's coming attractions." Albert Einstein

Checking In

How are you doing with these new ways of thinking? Have you been using them? Are you excited about the possibilities of what's to come and what is possible for you?

Working with your thoughts is the most effective way to replace the early childhood messages and conditioning you did not choose, so that you can then discover and create new ways of being.

Chapter 16

Replacing Patterns of Feelings and Actions

In the previous chapter we covered ways to replace patterns of thinking that came from the messages you grew up with and your life experiences. In this chapter, you'll learn how to replace patterns of feelings and patterns of actions.

Replacing Patterns of Feelings

Just like you were conditioned at a young age on how to think, you were also conditioned or told how to feel and what emotions were or were not acceptable. Or worse, you may have gotten the message that it wasn't okay to have emotions, and you suppressed them. Whether or not you feel your feelings or express your emotions, know that what you do is a pattern.

To replace the pattern of how you feel requires putting your attention on something that makes you feel different. This can be done through thought or experience. It doesn't matter how you do it—whether it is an actual experience or in your imagination, because the brain doesn't know the difference.

All it takes to shift a pattern of feeling is to focus on something that will give you the feeling you would rather experience. If you want to feel happy, think about what makes you happy or do something that gives you a happy feeling. If you want to feel relaxed, think about something relaxing, look at a relaxing image, or do something like deep breathing, yoga, or meditation.

Music can help create new patterns of feelings. Listening to upbeat, positive, or inspirational music may lift your mood. Calm music could help you feel relaxed, and sad songs may help you access suppressed emotions.

When you are feeling frustrated, angry, or resentful, it's not a bad thing. It may be just what you need to give you the energy to do something differently. The one rule I tell clients is that you can feel what you feel and do what you want as long as it does not cause harm to yourself, another person, an animal, or property. It's okay to be angry. It is okay to be sad or upset, because when we do not feel our feelings, they get stored in our bodies, and eventually, they leak out, causing an emotional outburst—or worse—an illness or disease.

Feeling your feelings is important for your well-being. The goal with feelings is to produce the feeling state you want to experience rather than the old feeling state or non-feeling state that has been your pattern.

Replacing Patterns of Actions

Doing, doing, doing. So much of what we do is based on our conditioning and the high value placed on productivity. It's no wonder that as adults, we often find ourselves doing what we "have to do," "should do," or think we are "supposed to do" rather than what we want to do or yearn to do.

A pattern of action can be modified or eliminated by changing how you do something or by not doing it at all. If there is something you don't like doing but feel that you must, it may be time for a break. That could look like taking some time off, negotiating a new agreement, or delegating a task.

Avoidance is a pattern of action. It's the act of not doing something. You may want a result, but for some reason, consciously or unconsciously, you don't put in the time and effort. You do not take the action necessary to achieve the outcome you would like.

The way to shift a pattern of avoidance is to engage in an action that would get you your desired result. Start with anything—just one little thing toward what you want. By knowing your desired outcome, you can adjust your thoughts and feelings to be congruent with it.

It takes repetition to change any pattern, especially lifelong patterns. Be patient as you practice replacing old patterns with more effective ones.

Repeating Patterns

Max, age fifty, felt dissatisfied and bad about himself because he was not where he thought he would be in his life by now. He didn't understand why he couldn't get his life together. As a result, he often got down on himself and berated himself, wondering why he wasn't motivated to make changes.

Max had no clue that how he felt about himself and his struggles came from generations of those who came before him with similar struggles. He learned that change is difficult because the familiar feels safe, and he had gotten used to being comfortably uncomfortable. Although he felt dissatisfied, he knew how to survive in this familiar place.

We all have stories of repeating the same patterns, of having the same experiences, the same types of problems, and the same interactions with people. These are predictable reoccurrences based on how we view ourselves and others.

Stubborn, Controlling, and Passive

In my formative years, I learned to become overly responsible. As I carried out the pattern of being overly responsible. Without realizing it, I was rigid in my ways of what "had" to be done and how it was done—thoroughly and perfectly, just like my mother taught me. This meant I could not be flexible, creative, and open to new or different ways of living and doing things.

I also learned not to express myself or speak up. And because I took on the pattern of being passive, I have tended to go along with what others decided.

Stubborn, controlling, or passive is not who we are; it is how we became from our early childhood conditioning of how to be and how not to be.

Disconnected from Ourselves

When we are disconnected from our feelings, needs, wants, and desires, we are disconnected from ourselves. We stay in this pattern for various reasons, mainly because to change or to feel our feelings seem scary. It is the unknown that we fear, when we don't know what something will be like or feel like.

The idea of changing can have your mind swirling with doubts and fears like:

What if I don't like what I thought I wanted?
What if my life gets worse and not better?
What if they don't like or accept me?

Expect to Ruffle Some Feathers

By thinking, feeling, and acting differently, you will be making some changes, and people who have become accustomed to how you have been might not like that you are no longer making them a priority or tending to them like you used to.

There may be an adjustment or a renegotiation that needs to occur as you value yourself and say no at times while making some much-needed changes for you to feel good and live the life you desire.

You deserve to enjoy your life just as much as others.

You deserve to enjoy your life just as much as others.

Chapter 17

Defining You!

If you are like most adults, your early childhood programming and experiences have defined you, and not in a good way. Now, you get to define who you are and how you want to be.

Imagine who you would be today...

If growing up, you had permission to explore and learn about your environment and yourself
If you grew up hearing affirming, reassuring, and validating words
If you felt supported and loved

From the time we were little children, we have been trained to give too much of ourselves. Girls especially were raised to give, serve, nurture, and care for others. These are great qualities when they are in balance with giving them to yourself as well. Unfortunately, as adults, most of our energy goes one way—giving, doing, and working for others. Whether out of duty, obligation, necessity, or to make a living, we have been conditioned to neglect ourselves.

So many of us do not give it a second thought as we work hard, give until we have nothing else to give, and think running on empty is normal. It's no wonder we feel stuck and low on energy.

It is not too late to make up for the deficits from childhood. You can learn to give to yourself in ways that feel caring, nurturing, and loving to you.

It is not too late to make up for the deficits from childhood. You can learn to give to yourself in ways that feel caring, nurturing, and loving to you.

It's Okay to Feel and Have Needs

The first step in defining yourself is to know yourself. This means getting in touch with some of your feelings and preferences—needs, wants, wishes, desires, and dreams.

To get to know yourself better, ask yourself questions like these:

How do I feel about this situation?
What do I want instead?
What do I need?
If I did have a desire or preference, what would it be?
If I did feel my feelings, what would I be feeling right now?

The more you know yourself, the easier it will be to let go of who you have been (from your childhood conditioning) to become the person you want to be.

Expectations

A belief of what might happen is more powerful than an expectation. We all have beliefs and expectations, whether we are aware of them or not. We may want or expect something and not be aware that we don't believe it could happen.

Our beliefs may sound like this:

Who am I kidding?
Who am I to _____?
That will never happen.
I don't deserve that.
I'm too _____. (For example, I'm too young or I'm too old.)

As much as we might want something better, it's common for people *not* to believe or expect a situation at work, at home, or with their family to improve. Change may feel scary. The unknown is unpredictable, and we tend to like staying with what is familiar. Not expecting something to improve also keeps us from getting our hopes up, only to be disappointed.

What beliefs or expectations are you aware of that you would like to change?

Look for What Is Right

It's easy to find fault, mainly because that's how humans have functioned as problem-focused beings needing to assess for safety. As we shift out of survival mode, we can look for what is right with ourselves and others.

Focusing on flaws and traits we don't like in ourselves prevents us from seeing what is good and right with us. When we focus on positive aspects, which we all have, we will see a different side of ourselves. That is when our relationship with ourselves will improve for the better.

In the following chapter, we will look at how you view yourself, which is the basis for defining who you are and who you want to become.

Chapter 18

How You See Yourself

Early childhood messages negatively or positively shape our self-image, self-esteem, self-worth, and self-confidence. Negative messages and experiences in childhood create adults who have challenges handling adversity. In contrast, positive messages and experiences produce adults who handle life's challenges more easily.

We can know what to do, think we feel confident, and not reach or obtain a goal. The disappointment or rejection can feel unfair, but deep down we may feel undeserving, unworthy, or incapable, and it may not feel safe to go against our deeply ingrained early childhood messages.

In this chapter, I will walk you through how you developed your self-concept and identity, which then shaped your self-image, how you view and treat yourself, and ultimately, how you live your life.

Now would be a great time to get some paper or your journal so that you can take some notes on how you see yourself.

Self-Concept

A self-concept develops in childhood from messages, experiences, and conclusions of who we think we are. Our self-concept is made up of how we see ourselves, think about ourselves, and feel about ourselves.

Some common negative conclusions we come to about ourselves are:

I'm not good enough.
I'm not deserving.
I'm worthless.
I'm stupid.
I'm unlovable.

Some positive conclusions we come to about ourselves are:

I am a kind person.
I am a good friend.
I am worthy.
I am smart.
I am deserving.

Our self-concept is comprised of both negative and positive conclusions we came to about ourselves.

Identity

From our self-concept, we developed an identity. Our identity is how we see and define ourselves.

Part of your identity may include mixed thoughts like these:

I'm not good at math.

I'm outgoing.

I pride myself on being able to do without.

I am responsible, and people can count on me.

Your identity may be defined by being similar to people you admire or look up to, or it may be the opposite of not wanting to be like specific people such as your mother, father, sister, or brother… who have or had ways of being that you decided weren't how you wanted to be.

Self-Image

A self-image is how we perceive ourselves. It's a series of self-impressions that have built up over time. These impressions can be very positive, giving a person confidence in their thoughts and actions, or negative, making them doubtful of their capabilities and ideas.

Our self-image is based on our perceptions of reality. It's built over a lifetime and continues to change as we do, and it is something we have some influence over. Our self-image has a lot to do with our self-esteem. After all, how we see ourselves is a big contributing factor to how we feel about ourselves.

A positive self-image includes:

Seeing yourself as an attractive and desirable person.

Having an image of yourself as a smart and intelligent person.
Seeing a happy, healthy person when you look in the mirror.
Believing that you are at least somewhat close to your ideal version of yourself.
Thinking that others perceive you as all the above as well as yourself.

A negative self-image is the flipside of the above; it looks like this:

Seeing yourself as unattractive and undesirable.
Having an image of yourself as a stupid or unintelligent person.
Seeing an unhappy, unhealthy person when you look in the mirror.
Believing that you are nowhere near your ideal version of yourself.
Thinking that others perceive you as all the above as well as yourself.

A poor self-image can be a significant factor in producing depression. When we feel bad about ourselves, it's natural that our perception of ourselves is low.

Self-Esteem

Self-esteem is how we feel about ourselves, specifically how valuable or worthwhile we feel. It's the overall feeling of respect for ourselves and our abilities and involves how much we like ourselves. It is our overall sense of personal value and self-worth.

How we feel about ourselves is significant when we consider that our feelings are preceded by our thoughts about how we see ourselves (our self-image) and how we describe ourselves (our identity).

A person with low self-esteem tends to have a lack of respect or dislike for themselves. A negative self-image influences self-esteem, and having low self-esteem is likely to be accompanied by a negative self-image. Additionally, having a negative self-image and low self-esteem includes having low self-worth and a lack of self-confidence.

Now would be a good time to think about or write about the messages you grew up with and how they have influenced your identity, self-image, and self-esteem.

What follows next are additional ways we may see or treat ourselves.

Self-Worth

Having a sense of self-worth means that we value ourselves, and having a sense of self-value means that we are worthy. Self-worth is at the core of our very selves. Our thoughts, feelings, and behaviors are intimately tied to how we view our worthiness and value as human beings.

Having a realistic view of ourselves and our abilities can help us have a sense of self-worth. So can knowing that our worth as a human is not dependent on our ability to perform, compete, achieve, or produce anything. It is also not based on how we look, what we own, how much we earn, what we do for work, or our relationship status.

Many of us grew up pleasing others and learned to base our self-worth on the happiness of others. When determining your self-worth, consider your kindness, compassion, empathy, respect for others, and how well you treat those around you.

We all have flaws and are imperfect, and we do not have to buy into the voice in our heads that says we are unworthy. We can feel intelligent, talented, and successful even if we are not the best, smartest, or most talented. Doing so allows us to have a healthy level of self-worth.

As human beings, we are worthy of being loved, respected, and appreciated. As children, most of us were taught that our value comes from what we do and not from who we are. Having successful experiences is a way to gain a healthy sense of self-worth because it boosts our sense of competency and mastery, making us feel good about ourselves. Self-acceptance and self-compassion also contribute to having a sense of self-worth.

Selfish

When someone says, "You are being selfish," it can produce feelings of guilt and shame. "Don't be selfish" is something many of us heard growing up. It is a message instilled in us from a young age and can cause an inner conflict when we need to care for ourselves.

A selfish person is someone who is concerned excessively or exclusively with their interests regardless of others. They lack consideration for others while seeking or concentrating on their own advantage, pleasure, or well-being. People considered selfish might be labeled egotistical, narcissistic, inconsiderate, self-absorbed, self-centered, self-obsessed, self-preoccupied, or self-serving.

The message is loud and clear: "You are paying too much attention to your wants and needs and not enough attention to others." Another message you may have heard is: "A good person thinks of others first."

We don't have to look too far to see people struggling with physical and mental health because they do not take adequate care of themselves. In many cases, the root cause can be linked to their early childhood programming to be selfless, or worse, self-sacrificing, which means giving everything to others and sacrificing their own needs.

Taking care of ourselves puts us in a better position to do things that benefit others. It's a win/win situation. The better we feel, the more we have to give to our family, friends, work, and community.

Self-Sacrifice

Self-sacrifice is, in essence, living for others and not for ourselves. It's accommodating others, dropping everything for whoever "needs" us, and paying little attention to our own feelings and needs. It's giving to family and friends, putting in the effort at work, and telling ourselves things like, "Of course, I can do that for you." Or "I can go without. You need it more than I do."

When we come from a place of self-sacrifice, we are putting our psychological health at risk. People who neglect their own needs are more likely to experience anxiety, depression, emotional exhaustion, low productivity, and burnout. There may also be physical health consequences due to lowered immunity.

People who self-sacrifice may have grown up with a parent who acted like a martyr, selflessly taking care of everyone else but not attuned to their feelings and needs; thus, healthy limits and boundaries were not modeled. They may have also had parents, grandparents, teachers, or religious leaders who encouraged and praised self-sacrificing behavior and made them feel guilty if they were not thinking about others over and above themselves.

Also, growing up with authoritarian parents who were domineering and controlling can predispose a child to become a self-sacrificing adult. A parent who routinely got angry, upset, or emotionally pulled away from their child if they did not do things their way can cause the child to sacrifice their own needs.

We need to be able to say no to something or someone and listen to our feelings (such as frustration) that tell us when "enough is enough." Otherwise, at some point we end up feeling angry, bitter, and resentful.

Three healthy messages to embrace to end self-sacrificing behaviors are:

My needs are just as important as others.
I do not give at the expense of myself.
Giving to others is a joy when I have attended to my own needs first.

Self-Doubt

Self-doubt is having a lack of faith in ourselves and feeling uncertain about our abilities, thereby doubting our competence, worth, and personal value. The higher our level of self-doubt, the lower our self-esteem. When we doubt ourselves, our focus is on our inability to succeed and the bad things that might happen as a result of failing.

Self-doubt may stem from previous negative experiences or from being criticized in childhood. Messages like "you're not good enough" or being made to feel incapable can produce self-doubt.

Self-doubt can cause a lack of motivation, self-sabotage, and anxiety. Equally distressing, self-doubt may lead to overachievement and striving to perform beyond one's capabilities to overcome the fear of failing or prove to others a level of ability to gain or maintain social or professional approval.

A certain level of self-doubt is normal, especially when learning a new skill, and it may prevent us from being overconfident or complacent. At its core, self-doubt is how we view ourselves and who we believe ourselves to be. Self-doubt can interfere with trying in the first place, especially when we don't believe we can attain the result we want. Self-doubt will also get in the way of persevering in the face of challenges.

Self-Criticism

Self-criticism is typically experienced as negative internal thoughts about oneself or, more specifically, about one's behaviors or attributes. Chronic or excessive self-criticism can get in the way of taking appropriate risks, asserting opinions, or believing in our abilities and may contribute to mental health concerns, such as depression, anxiety, body image issues, or feelings of worthlessness. Blaming oneself when things go wrong may lead to feelings of failure or a depressed mood.

Overly self-critical individuals may feel guilty or ashamed when something goes wrong, believing it's their fault. Self-criticism has been linked with perfectionism, self-harm, and eating and food issues.

Self-criticism can also lead to projecting negative beliefs onto others, resulting in the expectation of outside criticism or negative feedback. When negativity and strong criticism or extreme disapproval is expected, interpersonal relationships may be negatively impacted. Internal and external criticism can lead to loneliness and isolation and contribute to a person's withdrawal from others. A self-critical individual may also find it challenging to assert their needs and desires and are more likely to exhibit submissiveness in relationships with others out of fear that voicing an opinion will lead to criticism.

When self-critical thoughts are applied broadly rather than focused on a particular behavior, they may be more likely to negatively impact well-being, and produce thoughts like:

I'm a failure.
I can't do anything right.
I'm not good enough.
I'll never get better.

The above statements do not focus on any particular behavior that can be improved. Instead, they apply a negative mindset in an all-encompassing manner and may be more likely to affect confidence and contribute to developing physical and mental health concerns.

Specific acknowledgments would sound like these:

I stayed up so late last night. I know I feel my best when I get more sleep.
I watched TV and didn't study for my exam. I don't like feeling unprepared.
I scolded my son too harshly. Next time I will talk to him calmly.
If I keep speeding, I might hurt someone or get a ticket. I know I need to slow down.

These statements focus on a particular aspect of behavior that can be improved. The statements are honest and constructive rather than negative. Honest, specific self-criticism will likely lead to improved behavior and modifications of perceived shortcomings.

Excessively self-critical thoughts often have their roots in negative experiences with parents and primary caregivers in childhood. For example, an authoritarian parenting style, which is parenting with control and rigidity, may foster negative self-perceptions and a low sense of self-worth in children. When children feel rejected by their parents, are not treated with warmth and compassion, or are frequently criticized, they may be more likely to grow up overly critical of themselves and others.

When parents give children autonomy, encourage them to attempt things for themselves, and allow them to make mistakes without strong criticism or excessive disapproval, children are more likely to develop self-confidence and grow up with a sense of security regarding their own choices.

Self-Judgment

Self-judgment is judging ourselves as bad, wrong, or inadequate and is one of the significant causes of fear, anger, anxiety, and depression. Most of us don't realize that these painful feelings result from our own thoughts and self-judgments. Remember that critical thoughts came from what we heard and made meaning from in our early childhood years. As we repeat critical thoughts to ourselves, they can feel like they are ours, but they did not originate with us.

Generally, we judge ourselves in the hope of protecting ourselves against rejection and failure. We falsely believe statements like these: "If I judge myself, then others won't judge me or reject me." "I can be safe from others' judgment by judging myself first," or "If I judge myself, I can motivate myself to do things right and succeed. Then I will feel safe and be loved and accepted by others."

Self-judgment can also lead to regrets, missing out, and hiding. An example is not liking the way you look in a swimsuit. A person who does not like the way their body looks tends to hide their body, which leads to missing out on experiences and having regrets. A conflicting thought sounds like this: "I want to enjoy the water on vacation with my kids, but I don't want to be seen in a swimsuit."

Judgment and criticism are often used by adults to affect behavior in others. Instead of motivating us, these methods tend to hurt and immobilize people. Criticism often creates anxiety that stops us from taking appropriate action for ourselves and can increase self-judgment from a lack of action. Just as a child does far better in school with encouragement than with criticism, so do adults at work and at home.

Self-Blame

Self-blame magnifies our perceived inadequacies, whether real or imagined, causing us to feel worse about ourselves. Self-blame is taking responsibility and accusing ourselves of things that are not our fault. When we are self-blaming, it is often because we were conditioned from an early age to take responsibility and ownership for things that were not ours to carry. We might have been part of a family whose dysfunction we absorbed and took on as our own.

Children develop self-blame as a way of coping with situations that are extreme and feel dangerous. These include experiencing mental, emotional, or physical abuse and interpreting it as their fault. Or having been traumatized so deeply that they learned to devalue themselves and blame themselves for their own trauma.

Taking on blame that is not ours can be an effective way to calm another person when we are in a volatile situation. It may be a good coping strategy to escape a dangerous situation, but it is not a recommended habit.

Nothing Good Comes from Feeling Bad about Ourselves

Feeling bad about ourselves does not correct a situation, solve a problem, teach new skills, or provide new opportunities or possibilities. Rather, it causes a downward spiral of thoughts and feelings. Fears and worries, guilt and shame, anger, resentment, sadness, and depression—none of these will improve a situation. Feeling bad about ourselves creates distance and a negative self-view as someone who is powerless.

The view we have of ourselves determines how we live our lives. A negative self-view sets us up to struggle as we navigate life with self-doubt, self-judgment, and self-blame. Having a negative self-view may feel familiar, but it will prevent you from developing self-confidence, self-respect, and self-acceptance.

A more solid sense of self can be developed by replacing how we have been labeled and defined, generally by sources outside of ourselves. In the next chapter are positive self-views that will move you toward feeling good about yourself.

Chapter 19

Positive Self Views

In the previous chapter, you learned how your view of yourself was developed based on early childhood messages that negatively or positively shaped your self-image, self-esteem, and self-worth. Even if you have self-criticism or self-doubt, the positive self-views described in this chapter, when adopted, will help you view yourself more confidently and treat yourself with more kindness.

It's one thing to learn about different ways of thinking, feeling, and being; it's another to live it. As you begin to reshape your identity and view yourself more positively, have compassion for yourself. Remember, you are learning a new skill that will take practice before it becomes your natural way of being.

Without care and kindness for yourself, it's not possible to genuinely be happy and enjoy life. As you read through the positive self-views, imagine what it would be like to incorporate each one of them into your everyday way of life. How would you feel, and what would you be doing? Then select one or two positive self-views to integrate into your life.

Self-Compassion

Giving ourselves the same kindness and care we would give to a good friend is self-compassion. Many people extend compassion toward others but find it difficult to extend the same compassion toward themselves. They may see self-compassion as an act of self-indulgence, but extending compassion toward oneself is not an act of self-indulgence, selfishness, or self-pity.

Self-compassion is being warm and understanding toward ourselves when we feel inadequate, fail, or are having a rough time, instead of ignoring how bad we feel or beating ourselves up with self-criticism. Self-compassionate people know that being imperfect, failing, and experiencing life challenges are inevitable, so they are gentle with themselves when in a difficult situation.

Many mental health concerns, such as anxiety or insecurity, may be relieved with self-compassion, and high levels of self-compassion may positively impact recovery from post-traumatic stress. The painful thoughts and memories after a traumatic experience may be less threatening when self-compassion is sufficient and facing those experiences may be more manageable.

Another area where the benefit of self-compassion has been identified is with the prevention of compassion fatigue or caregiver burnout, which can occur from providing extensive care to others. Those who have as much compassion for themselves as for others are generally able to remain in touch with their own needs and maintain physical and mental well-being, commonly with the help of an essential self-care routine.

Kristin Neff, PhD, is the leading expert on self-compassion, and she goes deep into this topic in her book *Self-Compassion: Stop Beating Yourself Up and Leave Insecurity Behind* (Neff 2015).

Self-Acceptance

Self-acceptance can be defined as 1) the awareness of one's strengths and weaknesses, 2) the realistic (yet subjective) appraisal of one's talents, capabilities, and general worth, and 3) feelings of satisfaction with oneself despite deficiencies and regardless of past behaviors and choices.

Self-acceptance is being satisfied or happy with oneself and is necessary for good mental health. Some psychological benefits of self-acceptance include mood regulation, decreased depressive symptoms, and increased positive emotions.

Other psychological benefits include:

A heightened sense of freedom
A decrease in fear of failure
An increase in self-worth
An increase in independence (autonomy)
An increase in self-esteem
Less desire to win the approval of others

Being less self-critical and kinder toward yourself when mistakes occur

Having more desire to live life for oneself (and not others)

Self-Care

Self-care is taking action to preserve or improve one's health, well-being, and happiness, especially in times of stress. Self-care is essential for physical, mental, emotional, and psychological well-being. Other benefits of self-care include fostering resilience, living longer, and becoming better equipped to manage stress.

Self-care is vital so we can be healthy, work, care for others, and do all the things we need, want, and desire to do each day. We need to replenish ourselves daily. Self-care is not selfish or self-indulgent. Self-care is essential!

When we don't do enough to take care of ourselves by getting adequate sleep, managing our stress, moving our bodies, consuming nutritious food and water, and doing things we enjoy—that's when our bodies break down, and we don't have the bandwidth to keep up. We may find ourselves anxious or depressed, burned out, or with an illness.

Self-care is vital so we can be healthy, work, care for others, and do all the things we need, want, and desire to do each day.

We need to replenish ourselves daily. Self-care is not selfish or self-indulgent. Self-care is essential!

Self-Trust

Learning to trust ourselves is one of the most important things we can do to create the life we want. Everyone has an internal compass, and following it is always the best path to long-term happiness. The problem is that most of us have been conditioned to second-guess ourselves and put our trust in others.

Self-trust means staying true to ourselves and trusting our judgment and abilities. It means sticking to personal standards, ethics, and core values. It is pursuing our dreams without letting others stop us.

People who are self-trusting have clarity and confidence in their choices. They are interdependent, which includes healthy dependency, not overly dependent or hyper-independent. They speak with authority that comes from deep within but is not arrogant. They are good observers and have cultivated the ability to learn from their experiences, both successes and failures.

Developing self-trust can be challenging for adults raised by parents who regularly swooped in to fix their problems. This can lead to difficulties handling responsibilities as an adult and feeling helpless or giving up when things get tough.

Past shaming or punishment by parents can also lead to not trusting ourselves. You've probably heard the phrase, "Children should be seen and not heard." If you were routinely punished or shamed for expressing your needs as a child, you're most likely carrying guilt, shame, or fear, and have a hard time trusting yourself.

On a grander scale, family, community, and society put pressure on who we should be, and it can feel uncomfortable, even dangerous, to express ourselves authentically.

Here is what a lack of self-trust looks and feels like:

Hiding your authentic self or feeling overly self-conscious.
Following the advice of an external authority, even when it's harmful to you.
Coming down hard on yourself when criticized, feeling guilty and ashamed.
Having difficulty making decisions and constantly asking others for guidance.
Being afraid of making the wrong choice or disappointing others.

When we don't trust ourselves, our actions often do not align with what matters to us. An inner conflict can develop between who we are and how we act. That is when we know we need to take control of our lives and learn how to trust ourselves.

Self-Confidence

Self-confidence is an attitude about our skills and abilities. Having self-confidence implies a personal sense of being capable and competent, and it is an ability that can be acquired and improved over time. Being self-confident means we accept and trust ourselves and have a sense of control in our life. A person with self-confidence knows their strengths and weaknesses and views themselves positively. They set realistic expectations and goals, communicate assertively, and can handle criticism.

On the other hand, having low self-confidence might make us feel full of self-doubt, be passive or submissive, or have difficulty trusting others. Low self-confidence has been associated with growing up in an unsupportive and critical environment, judging ourselves too harshly, and being afraid of failure. Someone lacking self-confidence may feel inferior, unloved, or sensitive to criticism. Feeling confident in ourselves might depend on the situation. For instance, we can feel very confident in our jobs but lack confidence in relationships.

Having high or low self-confidence is rarely related to our actual abilities and is mainly based on our perceptions. Perceptions are how we think about ourselves, and these thoughts can be flawed. Realistically appraising one's abilities enables people to strike a healthy balance between too little and too much confidence. Too little confidence can prevent people from taking risks and seizing opportunities in work, school, or social situations. Too much confidence can come off as arrogance or narcissism. Overestimating one's abilities might also lead to problems such as failing to complete projects on time.

Self-Respect

Self-respect is the belief that we are worthy of love, attention, and respect and we are no less than anyone else. Self-respect is having a sense of honor and dignity for ourselves and our choices. It is also the foundation for respecting everything else and everyone else.

Self-respecting people:

Consider themselves.
Value themselves.
Speak up for themselves.

When we respect ourselves, we know when to say no to what is not mentally, emotionally, or financially healthy for us.

A self-respecting person can recognize their strengths and limitations and view limitations as growth areas rather than permanent signs of failure. Conversely, a person without self-respect tolerates poor treatment and is quick to excuse it or believe they deserve it. This plays out in many ways. A person may be lied to, talked down to, ignored, or left out. It can happen to any of us, but the difference is that a self-respecting person would not accept this. They would set boundaries with others about how they will and will not be treated.

We may give a person a chance to explain, apologize, or change their behavior, and as someone with self-respect, we would unlikely let it happen again and again. A person who struggles with self-respect is likely to have trouble in their relationships— by not asserting themselves, being pushed around or taken advantage of, and being quite unhappy.

Lack of self-respect might sound like these statements.

I disrespect myself when:

I do too much for others.
I think of others' needs and not my own.
I don't tune in to know what I need.
I don't honor my needs.
I don't ask for what I want.

People inherently treat us as we instruct them to, and if we don't hold ourselves in high esteem, others will consciously or unconsciously not treat us respectfully either. Without self-respect, even the most well-meaning partner, who initially sees their loved one as deserving the best, will start to lose this vision and begin to see and treat their partner only as well as the person values themself.

When we have self-respect, it's easier to live by our values and accept responsibility for our actions and choices because they are based on what is important to us. Doing so allows us to have more genuine and fulfilling relationships with others. Ultimately, our relationships with family, friends, and loved ones can be positively affected and more authentic.

Self-Love

Self-love is giving ourselves the unconditional love we didn't get. Having a high regard for our well-being and happiness means taking care of our own needs and not sacrificing our well-being to please others. Self-love means not settling for less than we deserve.

Self-love means accepting ourselves as we are in this very moment. It means accepting our emotions for what they are and putting our physical, emotional, and mental well-being first.

Self-love means accepting ourselves as we are in this very moment. It means accepting our emotions for what they are and putting our physical, emotional, and mental well-being first.

Being kind, patient, gentle, and compassionate to ourselves the way we would with someone else we care about is an act of self-love. Truly caring for ourselves and making room for healthy habits is self-love. It's doing things not to "get them done" or because we "have to" but because we care about ourselves.

Self-love can be:

Prioritizing yourself
Listening to your body
Talking to and about yourself in a caring way
Setting healthy boundaries
Taking breaks from work, eating well, and moving and stretching your body
Doing something enjoyable or creative
Forgiving yourself when you're not being true or nice to yourself

Self-Reliance

First, I want to say what self-reliance is not. It's not about doing everything ourselves. It's not about being financially independent either. And it is certainly not about shouldering every hardship we face alone. Self-reliance is not about cutting ourselves off from everybody or isolating ourselves from society.

Self-reliance is the ability to think autonomously by trusting our instincts, embracing our individuality, and striving toward our goals. It's being true to ourselves, capable of independent thought, knowing what we want, and pursuing what we want independently of others' judgments. Self-reliance means we can solve problems and make decisions independently.

As a self-reliant person, you would feel happy by yourself, in yourself, and about yourself—without needing to rely on others. Self-reliance gives us authority and agency over our lives.

Chapter 20

Being True to Yourself

There is a time to compromise, adapt, accommodate, and defer to others, but we are not being true to ourselves if this is our primary pattern of interacting. When we give up too much of ourselves to others, we become disconnected from who we are and what is most important to us.

As children, we learned what was acceptable and what was not acceptable, and we adapted to survive. We also based our value and worth on the reactions and responses of others—whether they approved or disapproved of us, whether they were happy with us or unhappy with us.

We were not taught to know ourselves and to follow our desires. Being true to ourselves means recognizing our needs and not dismissing them. It means having respect for ourselves and our desires. It's being congruent with who we are.

Most of the people I work with focus more on others than on themselves. The concept of being true to themselves is foreign because they haven't learned how to get beyond the childhood messages that went against this concept. I, myself, have spent most of my adulthood doing what I learned to do—setting myself aside, being good, staying quiet, and doing what was expected of me. My brain was wired to put others first, and these were my survival mechanisms.

If you notice yourself feeling stressed and overwhelmed on a regular basis, exhausted most of the time, or angry and resentful—you are not being true to yourself. When we are not true to ourselves, it takes a toll on us mentally, emotionally, physically, and spiritually.

Feeling significant and being true to yourself is essential for your health, happiness, and well-being.

Feeling significant and being true to yourself is essential for your health, happiness, and well-being.

The Price I Paid for Not Being True to Myself

In 2005, I was near burnout in every area of my life. I was working twelve to fourteen hours a day in private practice doing child custody work. And as a "good" wife and mother, I did the best I could to tend to my husband, our two daughters, and our dog and cat—taking care of everyone else because that was what I was "supposed to do."

There came a moment when I realized I couldn't live like this anymore. I had lost myself and had nothing more to give. My ability to focus was declining along with my health. All of the things I used to do for self-care slowly slipped by the wayside as I took on more and more work. My life was way out of balance.

I didn't realize the extent of what giving too much of myself had on me until I stopped. I took some time off work, and during the first six months I went at my own pace and let myself be as I recovered from doing way too much. I gardened, did jigsaw puzzles, cooked, went on walks with friends, and played games with my kids. I did things that brought me joy and happiness.

As I considered my future, I knew I never wanted to "give up me" and live from my deeply ingrained childhood conditioning like that again. Being overly responsible, putting others first and taking care of everyone else at the expense of my own needs was what I knew how to do, and that was not how I wanted to live. I needed to be "in my life" and balance my needs along with the needs of my family.

Lifelong patterns may take some time to replace, so be gentle with yourself. It can be challenging to balance the needs of others while staying true to what you want and what fulfills and sustains you if, as a child, you learned:

To do what you were told.

To put others and their happiness above yours.

That it's selfish to think of yourself and your needs.

Along my journey to discovering who I was, what I liked and what I didn't like, I learned to identify my early childhood programming, think differently, and live a more congruent life. This is the process I have been sharing with you throughout this book. It's empowering to intentionally choose the way you want to live, according to your beliefs and values.

Prioritizing Yourself

It may feel foreign or challenging to envision adding fun, enjoyable, and fulfilling activities to your daily life. Prioritizing yourself, even for a few minutes each day, can make a meaningful difference to becoming your true self.

Prioritize yourself with these suggestions:

Do something for you, even if it's for a few minutes. Before you give your time and energy to others, do something that makes you feel good. Get yourself ready for the day, eat a nutritious meal, do a workout, enjoy a cup of tea, or do anything else that adds to your well-being.

Pay attention to the signs your body is giving you to take care of it. You cannot be good to anyone else if your inner resources are depleted. Take a few minutes in the morning or afternoon to stretch, drink a glass of water, meditate, take some deep breaths, or go outside for a short walk.

Make a commitment to set limits and healthy boundaries where you say, "This is for me, and it's nonnegotiable." Block off your calendar to take a break, set a reminder on your phone to do an enjoyable activity, or schedule time to connect with people who make you happy.

When you make decisions that are right for you, regardless of what others might think or say, you are honoring and respecting yourself. The decisions you make may not be popular, and that's okay. It's up to you to find what fulfills and sustains you and then to prioritize that, unapologetically.

For example, I meditate every morning no matter what, even if it is for less time than I would prefer, because it's important for me to start my day feeling calm and connected to my inner self.

Saying No

Everyone struggles to say no occasionally. Depending on the situation, choosing *not* to say yes makes you stronger. By finding the courage to say no more often, you'll find that it gets easier over time. It also reduces the stress of committing to things you don't want to do.

No is a complete sentence. When saying no isn't enough, try one of these polite ways to turn someone or something down:

"No, I am not able to." (You don't need to offer a reason.)
"Thank you so much for inviting me, but I have other plans."
"I will have to check and get back to you." (Use this if you need some time to think about it.)

The next time you don't want to do something, rather than thinking you have to (old thinking) or feeling guilty if you don't (old feeling), be your true self and say no or "no, not this time."

Discover and Define What You Really Want

Most of us were conditioned *not* to let ourselves go after what we wanted. We have been living the limitations imposed on us. Just like the frogs in the jars that didn't jump out because they were conditioned to believe they couldn't after the lids were removed, we limit ourselves long after our metaphorical lids are removed.

As a result of our conditioning, we downplay our desires and set goals we think we can accomplish—playing it safe in our familiar comfort zone—and we don't get what we really want. We get more of what we don't want, which leads to feeling unsatisfied, disappointed, and bad about ourselves. Our limitations cause us to play small and believe we can't achieve or even pursue what we would really like.

In this section, I will guide you through some questions that will help you determine what you truly desire, even if you don't know how it could happen. You'll want to give yourself time to think about who you truly are beneath your childhood conditioning.

It's common *not* to know what you want if you learned not to have needs, wants, wishes, or desires. As you replace the generational messages passed down to you, expect to be curious about what you want. This is a process of unlearning old patterns, meeting your true self, and developing new beliefs.

Now would be a great time to get a pen and paper or a journal to write in as I take you through a series of prompts and questions. The purpose of these questions is to get you thinking about what *you* want or would like to improve.

Think about a situation or an area of your life that isn't the way you want it to be. What do you want instead?

If you aren't sure what you want, here are two prompts that may help you get clarity:

I prefer…
I would rather…

Allow yourself to dream about your desires in other areas of your life as you ask yourself these general questions:

- What would I like to experience?
- What would I like to do for the pure enjoyment of it?
- What would I enjoy doing for work (even if I did not get paid) because I love it so much?

When you know what you want, it gives you direction. When you show up for yourself every day with your wants, needs, wishes, and desires clearly defined, you are more likely to experience them.

Make a list of your top five desires.

Use this three-step process to give each of your desires the attention needed to fully connect with them:

1. Think about the outcome you really want. (Get a clear picture.)
2. Think about what could go right. (Possibilities of what could go right will outweigh limiting beliefs.)
3. Think about how good you will feel when it happens. (Feel it now.)

A few minutes spent connecting with what you truly desire, as if it has already happened, will keep you aligned with what you want. On a deeper level, your new thoughts and feelings will create neural pathways in your brain to replace your early childhood programming.

Chapter 21

Mental Resiliency

Being our best self enables us to welcome new experiences, ideas, and opportunities. That's when creativity leads to innovation, fun, excitement, and enjoyment of work and life. It also gives us the mental resilience to handle the challenges, disappointments, and losses that are part of life.

Mental resilience is having the ability to think clearly so we can consider options to deal with problems with our health, work, finances, relationships, or any other area of our lives.

Mental resilience allows us to do something different, take another direction, or take an alternative approach when something doesn't work out.

Mental resilience is having the ability to cope and adapt to change when times are tough.

Mental resilience allows us to tune into our thoughts and quiet the negative chatter that creates stress and anxiety and gets in the way of thinking clearly.

The good news is that mental resilience can be learned. It's within our human nature to be resilient and to be able to face the stressors and challenges of life. Developing resilience can help us cope and bounce back after changes, challenges, setbacks, disappointments, and failures.

How well do you cope?

How do you respond when the unexpected happens?
How do you react when you are faced with a new challenge?
How is it for you when you hear about distressing world events?

Here is what tends to happen to us in challenging times. We have a thought about the situation, which leads to a feeling. It can happen in an instant. We may feel it in our body as stress, tension, or a punch in the gut. Keep in mind, it's our thoughts about what is happening that determine how we feel.

Our feeling about a situation depends solely on the meaning we give to that event. And the meaning we give to an event is based on our past experiences or lack of experience with what is happening. We either have had a positive experience, a negative experience, or no experience to draw upon.

A person faced with a situation similar to one they have previously overcome might say to themselves, "I've got this. I can handle this." Whereas someone who had a negative experience might say, "I can't go through this again." And a person with no prior experience might say, "I don't know what to do."

Mentally, it makes a difference how we think about a situation. If our first thought is one of self-judgment, like, "It's all my fault," "I can't do anything right," or "I'm a loser." Or "There's something wrong with me," that is not helpful in figuring out a more favorable outcome.

We must learn new ways of thinking, being, and behaving if we want a different outcome. Otherwise, we will continue to reinforce the meaning we made in childhood about how we think about and handle difficult situations.

Mental Chatter

Think about what you tend to say to yourself when faced with an uncomfortable, unknown, or traumatic situation. It's one thing to have a fleeting thought, but when we encounter something uncomfortable, unknown, or traumatic, we don't have just one thought, and then it goes away. No, we tend to worry and think of worst-case scenarios or blame or criticize ourselves or others. I call this mental chatter.

Mental chatter keeps us in fear, anger, disbelief, stress, and anxiety, and the thoughts that create these feelings prevent us from being resilient.

When we spend time worrying, ruminating, thinking of worst-case scenarios, blaming, or criticizing, it prevents us from being resilient and using our creative minds in solution-focused ways.

Mental chatter keeps us in fear, anger, disbelief, stress, and anxiety, and the thoughts that create these feelings prevent us from being resilient.

Mental chatter prevents us from:

Keeping a positive view of ourselves
Thinking clearly and considering options
Having access to thoughts to do something different or to go in another direction when something doesn't work out
Coping and adapting to change when times are tough
Warding off physical ailments caused by negative thoughts, including aches, pains, poor digestion, and a weakened immune system, to name a few

When we are in a negative frame of mind, it decreases our ability to meet our body's health needs. With limited mental resources, we are likely to make poor food choices, skip exercising, and have difficulty sleeping.

Interrupting mental chatter is the key to freeing ourselves from the thoughts that keep us from being happy, healthy, and more resilient. Listening to or watching an interesting or uplifting interview, YouTube video, or podcast is a great way to fill our minds with something positive. Reading a quote, a passage, or a chapter in a book with a positive message will replace negative mental chatter, filling our minds with new possibilities.

Going through tough times can make us stronger if we learn new ways of thinking and coping. Otherwise, tough times can be seen as another setback or disappointment, reinforcing negative thoughts.

Mental Resilience

There are several common traits that mentally resilient people possess. They are being happy, flexible, patient, and optimistic. Each trait uniquely contributes to the ability to handle life's ups and downs more easily. Together, these traits provide a solid foundation, not only to weather life's storms but to thrive.

Let's take a look at each trait, along with suggestions on how to develop a greater level of them.

Happy

Being happy is a feeling of joy, pleasure, or contentment. Feeling happy is being delighted, pleased, or glad over a particular thing or outcome.

Happiness can be increased by looking for what makes you happy and keeping a Happiest Moment of the Day Journal where each night, you write three to five of the happiest moments of your day in a notebook.

Flexible

Having flexibility is adapting to different circumstances or dealing with changes. Flexibility includes considering what is possible, gaining a new perspective, and being open to something different.

Increase your mental flexibility by getting out of your routines and comfort zone, by trying new activities or hobbies, traveling to experience new cultures and cuisines, or exploring a new area nearby to walk, shop, or play.

Patient

Being patient is the ability to wait, accept, or tolerate frustration, delay, trouble, or suffering without getting angry, upset, or quitting. It's also the ability to stay calm while waiting for your turn or an outcome.

Increase your ability to be patient by slowing down, anticipating obstacles, and accepting "what is." Practice being patient with yourself and others by staying present in stressful or inconvenient situations.

Optimistic

Being optimistic is having a disposition or tendency to look on the more favorable side of events or conditions and expect the best outcome.

To increase your level of optimism, reflect on positive aspects of your life and the things that are going well. Read an inspiring quote or story or recall a time when an outcome turned out better than you expected or when you conquered a challenge.

Happiness Is the Antidote to Doubts and Fears

Happy thoughts over time will produce a happier you! The benefits of being happy are many—including fewer doubts and fears from survival thinking. When we have thoughts that create a happy feeling, we are more likely to be in touch with what we want and take steps to acquire it because we are not in survival mode.

When we have doubts and fears, our thoughts are about what we don't want. These include what could go wrong, possible disappointments, failures, and past experiences that did not go well.

Being in a state of happiness allows us to believe that it's possible to do, have, create, or experience something we want. When we are happy, content, hopeful, and inspired, ideas and creative solutions come to us.

Building on Our Strengths

While life has not been easy—and at times it has been downright awful with setbacks and challenges—we are still here and have a life to live. We survived childhood, which was no easy feat for many of us.

With all that we have been through in our lives, we have strengths that have gotten us through tough times. Many of our strengths were developed from our challenges. Regardless of how we acquired them, we each have strengths and can build upon them without experiencing more difficulties.

Our strengths include unique capabilities, talents, and characteristics that serve us well in difficult situations and in everyday life. Think of a time when you overcame a challenge, persevered, or were courageous. Your inner strengths are there, and we are going to build on them.

It's time to identify your strengths. Take a moment to recall times when you felt smart, creative, happy, or successful at something. It can be anything, big or small.

Now, make a list of the following:

Things you are good at
Your accomplishments
Strengths you have demonstrated when times were tough
Positive traits people have recognized in you or things they said you are good at

These are your natural strengths, your gifts, and talents. Embrace them and find ways to incorporate them into your personal and work life.

One way to show up as your best self is to remind yourself of times when you operated from your strengths instead of from your childhood conditioning.

It's not bragging or boasting to acknowledge and share times when you felt really good about yourself. It sets the tone for more great things.

It's not bragging or boasting to acknowledge and share times when you felt really good about yourself. It sets the tone for more great things.

Here's to you being your capable, amazing, incredible self!

Part 4

Living and Working Together

Chapter 22

Healthy Relationships

Y ou might be wondering what a healthy relationship is and how you can have one when you didn't grow up in one and don't have a clue how to be in one?

Healthy, committed relationships by definition are mutually beneficial, supportive, and respectful to both parties—where you support one another while having your own individual emotions, reactions, and processes.

A healthy relationship is less about "the relationship" and more about what you bring to the relationship or who you are in the relationship. When two people come together in any relationship, it is who they are that creates the relationship.

The key to a healthy relationship is to bring our best selves to the relationship instead of our conditioned child selves. When we find ourselves slipping back into old patterns, as we all do from time to time, we can pivot to a new thought about what we want rather than the old familiar one we don't want.

Here are some signs to let you know when your childhood conditioning is running:

Being disconnected from your feelings.
Being concerned about how others will react.
Feeling uncomfortable making decisions for yourself.
Being out of touch with what you need, want, or desire.
Doing what others say you "should" do.

Shift from old ways of thinking, feeling, and being by taking some time to discover how you want to show up so you can get back to being your best self.

We will have healthier relationships when we show up as a version of ourselves that has self-respect, self-compassion, self-trust, self-confidence, self-acceptance, and is self-reliant.

Healthy relationships are easier to maintain when each person has their own identity outside of the relationship. With a solid identity, we are less likely to fall back into old, conditioned patterns from childhood or feel responsible for our partner's happiness.

Allow Others to Find Their Way

We all have our histories and the reasons we do what we do—most of which came from our childhood conditioning and how we learned to cope. The journey to grow and evolve is ours to make, either by choice or by circumstances. As you think in new ways, know that it might include taking a step back and allowing others to find their way.

It may be foreign to focus on yourself—and that is your task.

Here are some questions to ponder if you tend to put a lot of attention on others:

What would it be like to allow others to live their lives and make decisions for themselves without meddling in their business or giving advice, especially when it is not asked?

How might it be to have care, compassion, and encouragement for others and trust that everyone is right where they are supposed to be on their journey?

What would it be like to let others experience their feelings and not step in to make it better for them or so that you feel more comfortable?

What would happen if you allowed children, teens, and adults to make mistakes as they learn?

The benefits of focusing on ourselves are that we get to take charge of our thoughts and our lives. The benefits to others—when we don't try to fix, rescue, or prevent them from making mistakes or struggling—are that they get to figure things out for themselves. They get to learn and grow while developing experience and resilience as they take charge of their lives.

If this is all new, be patient with yourself as you figure out who you want to be and how you want to show up in your relationships.

Here are some ways of speaking that will help you and the people you are close to be heard, seen, acknowledged, loved, and supported:

I could use _____ (an ear, a hug, some help).
I just want you to listen.
Is now a good time for us to talk?
I have something important I want to share.
I appreciate you and value your feedback.
I want to hear what you have to say.
Tell me more.
Help me understand.
It's okay.
What would you like to do?
What do you prefer?

Speaking to our partners or loved ones with love, care, and support, while being our best selves, will create healthier relationships.

Interdependent Relationships

Interdependent relationships allow each individual to have their needs met and live their lives without sacrificing their values. A relationship where we feel that we are often putting our partner's needs ahead of our own or vice versa is a relationship that is out of balance and not genuinely interdependent. Compromising can help a couple achieve a balance between the needs of both parties, as long as one person does not consistently neglect their needs.

Interdependent relationships require effort, nurturing, and healthy boundaries. Gaining awareness of our own needs and goals is an important step toward reciprocity in relationships. A conscious decision to occasionally compromise or sacrifice for another person can be positive as long as it doesn't get in the way of the needs of the one doing the compromising.

Whereas codependence leads to seeking validation and acceptance from others, interdependence means finding acceptance within oneself and welcoming additional support from external sources. Achieving interdependence as a couple will take effort and compassion and can lead to a healthy and satisfying long-term relationship.

Prodependence

Prodependence is an alternative way of managing a relationship with someone with an addiction or mental illness. It's a more empathetic and compassionate way to approach the caregiving of loved ones. Prodependence replaces the stigma of codependence with positive expressions of love, removing blame and shame on the very ones who are proactively supporting a loved one who is struggling.

The prodependence model emphasizes effective connection with loved ones while at the same time developing and maintaining healthy boundaries and self-care techniques for caregivers rather than detachment. A person in a prodependent relationship will offer help when a loved one needs it but does not do tasks they could manage themself.

Prodependence is a normal and healthy attempt to remain connected to a loved one while facing extraordinarily difficult circumstances. With prodependence, there is no blame or shame, no sense of being wrong, and no language that pathologizes the caregiving loved one. Instead, there is recognition for the effort given, plus hope and useful instruction for healing. It is a more humanistic way of approaching support for both people.

Forgiveness Is for You

Forgiveness is a gift to free yourself. Forgiveness is defined as a deliberate decision to release feelings of resentment toward a person or group who has harmed you, regardless of whether they deserve your forgiveness.

Forgiveness is *not* letting someone off the hook for an offense against you. When you forgive, you do not gloss over or deny the seriousness of what happened. Forgiveness does not mean forgetting, nor does it mean condoning or excusing offenses. Forgiveness can help repair a damaged relationship if you choose. It does not obligate you to reconcile with the person who harmed you or release them from legal accountability.

Instead, forgiveness brings the forgiver peace of mind and frees them from anger and resentment. True forgiveness involves letting go of deeply held negative feelings. By doing so, it empowers you to recognize the pain you suffered without letting that pain define you, enabling you to heal and move on with your life.

An excellent place to start when considering forgiving someone else is to forgive yourself first. Forgive yourself because you deserve to be forgiven for being human and acting from the conditioning you were programmed with in your formative years.

Forgive yourself because the most important relationship you have is with yourself. Make peace with yourself. Whatever you did or think you did, whatever mistakes you made cannot be changed. It does you no good to treat yourself unkindly. Move on and create an identity that includes self-love rather than self-punishment.

Thoughtfulness

We live in a world where millions of people are struggling mentally, emotionally, physically, and financially. And because of their struggles and how they feel about themselves, they may be inattentive, uncaring, unkind, ill-mannered, impolite, rude, uncivil, malicious, mean, spiteful, inconsiderate, and thoughtless. It's not their fault. This is the outcome of the generational patterns passed down for centuries that have denied us a strong solid foundation to handle ourselves and our lives in healthier ways.

A little thoughtfulness can go a long way in modeling caring behavior, which may significantly improve our relationships with one another and may even cause another person to become more thoughtful. Being thoughtful is showing consideration for the needs or feelings of other people. It's being caring, attentive, polite, and kind. It's the small, thoughtful gestures that add up and make a big difference.

Here are some ways to express thoughtfulness:

Speak kind words.
Listen with interest.
Be respectful and considerate.
Write a note of thanks or appreciation.
Send a thoughtful card in the mail.
Bring or send someone flowers.
Offer prayers or well wishes.
Celebrate together.
Send a text saying, "I'm thinking of you," "How are you doing?" or "I love you."

Who do you know that could use a little thoughtfulness today?

Chapter 23

Impacting Change Collectively

Messages and expectations of others about how to be and how not to be, authoritarian parenting with little to no regard of the needs of children, and violence as a model of problem-solving has gotten us where we are today. These ways of living have created much suffering, denying us a life filled with joy, happiness, purpose, and satisfaction.

Collectively we have been ineffectively dealing with or avoiding problems that are too big to ignore. The problems we face have spiraled out of control. The "Band-aid" approach of treating symptoms has not worked to help people struggling with their circumstances—which has led to staggering rates of depression, anxiety, addiction, poor health, and suicide.

We have gotten so far away from coming together civilly to address and resolve what ails us worldwide. We are seeing the long-term effects of not getting along and not working together. The level of conflict in relationships, families, communities, and countries has caused many people to feel helpless and hopeless.

The way we have been living is unstable and unsustainable. When we stop trying to adapt to what's not working and take control of what we do have control over—our thoughts, feelings, actions, and the meaning we make of our experiences—is when we will live happier, healthier lives and thrive.

I believe the *big problems* we face will no longer exist when we individually do our part to replace survival thinking and living. Imagine a world where people didn't do what they think they "should do," "have to do," or are "supposed to do" but rather got their needs met without having to sacrifice their values and themselves.

Picture a world where adults and children are encouraged to be who they are as they explore their interests and passions that bring them joy and happiness. Imagine how you, your family, your community, and the world would benefit from each of us pursuing what we are uniquely gifted to do.

Instead of battling each other and ourselves—which are lose/lose situations—we could live in environments where we get along, lift each other up, and show care and concern for ourselves and others. Imagine having peaceful interactions, agreeing to disagree, and having kindness, compassion, and respect for one another.

We All Are Affected by the Struggling and Suffering of Others

The impact of people we know, and those we don't know, who are struggling affect us all. There is a cost to families and society when individuals are suffering.

When a family member is not doing well mentally, emotionally, or physically, it can drain family resources, including the energy of those who step in and tend to that person. Caregiving adults may have difficulty concentrating at work or need to take time off work to care for an ailing family member. Both adults and children often have to take on more responsibility when a family member is ailing.

Children are especially receptive to what is happening at home, even if they are not told there is a problem. In a home where a parent is physically or emotionally unavailable to their child because of their distress, the child may regress in behavior, have the inability to focus at school, or develop somatic symptoms like stomachaches.

Another area that puts stress on people is work. Work demands can be unsustainable, stressful, and exhausting, leading to impatience and irritability, negatively affecting relationships and parenting.

Worry, fear, uncertainty, more responsibility, financial strain—these all impact how we feel about ourselves, how we treat ourselves, and how we treat others. Whether you are the one struggling or others close to you are, it affects us all.

What Can We Do?

Just as you have been thinking differently and viewing yourself more positively—the answer to what we can do to impact change collectively is to continue replacing old survival ways of thinking and being that no longer work for us.

We must move beyond being more concerned about what others think about us than:

What we think of ourselves
What we want, need, or desire
What matters to us individually and collectively

When we don't consider ourselves, we are not in the driver's seat of our lives.

Anytime we are feeling bad or having negative thoughts is an excellent time to ask ourselves, "What else is possible?" "What can I do to feel better?" "What can I do to change this situation?"

The goal is to feel good.

We can choose to think differently. We can choose better, more empowering thoughts, and we can make new decisions—for ourselves, our families, and our communities. The impact of how we think, feel, and behave could have a massive positive influence on those around us.

It might take stopping, slowing down, or taking a break to determine what would be effective. It may not come naturally or easily to replace lifelong patterns every time. That's why it's important to become aware of your patterns and remind yourself that there are other ways of thinking about any pattern or situation. Sometimes all we need is a new perspective.

Having Enough to Give

People who live from their true self rather than their inauthentic conditioned self, have more to give because they live a more congruent life. Their internal resources allow them to be more patient, creative, productive, and able to contribute to society. These are the people we can count on, who make good leaders, and who come up with innovative ideas for solving current and future problems.

To have enough to give, we must first have our own needs met and not be bogged down with fears, worries, and the expectations of others. When we are living from our true selves and are confident and calm, we have the energy to give to others.

We are also more open to opportunities—noticing them and seeking them. We are more resourceful and open to new insights, perspectives, and possibilities. In this state of being, we have clearer thinking and are more likely to access our intuition, our sense of knowing what to ask or what to do next, and that allows us to make wise decisions.

Having Compassion

Knowing how most of us were raised, could you have more compassion for others? Might you wonder what types of childhood conditioning and experiences others have had that are causing them to behave in undesirable ways?

Having compassion doesn't mean you accept disrespectful, rude, or abusive behavior. It means you don't have to react with or internalize anger, hate, or other strong feelings. This allows you to remain calm and not be in survival mode. It means that you don't take on the victim role because it's not about you. It's about another human being who is having a difficult time because they are operating from their childhood conditioning and the meaning they made from their experiences.

The more we can offer understanding and kindness rather than judgment and criticism, the more we will see people of all ages become better versions of themselves.

Working Together

We are stronger together than apart. We can achieve more with others than by ourselves. When we work together, synergy happens. Synergy is the combined ability of a group of people that, when working together, is greater than the total capability achieved by each person working separately.

We can live like we don't need anyone, but the truth is we do need each other. Connection, belonging, feeling safe and secure, and getting our basic needs met of food, clothing, and shelter are possible for everyone when people band together.

Improving Relationships

The relationships we have with people close to us can be challenging for many reasons, including the way relationships were modeled in our formative years, the messages we got about how to be in relationships, and harmful or disrespectful experiences in prior or current relationships.

The first place to start improving relationships is with ourselves. The more we know about our early childhood programming and how we made meaning about relationships, the easier it will be to understand our relationships. When we take good care of ourselves we are better able to interact in calm, kind, and respectful ways. Our relationships will become easier when our inner resources are strong, when we are more resilient, and when we bring our confident, compassionate selves to the people we interact with.

Healthy, stable adults in respectful relationships create environments where everyone thrives at home and at work. Parents who are available, patient, and engaging are better able to provide the foundation children need to become resilient adults. For these outcomes to occur, two things need to happen. Adults need to 1) become happier and healthier individuals and 2) increase the number of positive experiences they and their children have. These will minimize adverse childhood experiences.

People of all ages would benefit from acknowledging these truths:

It's normal to feel disappointed when you cannot do or have something.
It's normal to feel sad over the loss of something or someone.
It's normal not to know how to do something until we learn how.
It's *not* normal to live with chronic stress or fear.

We can have compassion for ourselves and each other when we remember that most of us did not get what we needed growing up. Over time, as more and more of us improve our relationship with ourselves, the same skills will carry over into other relationships. As more people experience positive interactions with each other, future generations will have healthier relationships because of better role modeling of how people relate to each other.

Helping Others

How would it be if we gave each other what our parents and caregivers could not give us? Now that you know what it takes to feel good and that feeling good has significant benefits for yourself and others, it is time to help others so they can benefit too.

If we don't adopt new ways of interacting, we can expect to experience more of the same. Everyone's quality of life will improve when we support each other and work together to identify problems and create solutions—in families, neighborhoods, cities, and countries. We can support each other, collaborate, have fun, and agree to disagree when necessary.

Cocreation, collaboration, building resilience, having tolerance for differences, looking out for each other, being inclusive, focusing on strengths, looking for the good, and expecting positive outcomes, lead to fulfilling and satisfying lives and relationships.

A more sustainable way of living, working, and learning includes:

Supporting each other to become better people by ensuring their basic needs are met.
Involving individuals by allowing them to voice their thoughts, needs, ideas, and opinions.
Listening to understand rather than to reply.
Brainstorming ideas and possibilities without judgment.
Giving people a way to contribute and make a difference.
Setting intentions, making plans, and committing to see them through.
Acknowledging, encouraging, and celebrating each other.
Being a positive role model.
Being kind, checking in, inviting and including others.

Replacing unrealistic and unsustainable expectations we have been conditioned to live up to personally, professionally, and academically.

We all have a part to play in the transformation of humanity, shifting from living in survival mode to stable, sustainable living where everyone can thrive.

We can be positive role models for each other. There is a tremendous need for people of all ages to model the kind of thinking and behaviors that show others it's possible for them to feel good and believe in themselves too.

Become a teacher, coach, or mentor by supporting and encouraging others. Believe in others who may not believe in themselves yet. Having someone who believes in others can help them see their capabilities until they can believe in themselves.

If you don't know how to be a positive role model, pretend to be the role model you wish you had. Or step into the role of being happy, caring, compassionate, and giving, and you can't go wrong. It is a win/win!

Chapter 24

Vision for the Future

Imagine if we lived our lives individually and collectively with words like compassion, curiosity, and respect, where trust is built and maintained and adults and children feel safe, supported, respected, and valued. In this final chapter you will find Words to Live By—words that provide a common language to create a thriving world. Each of the following words have been selected to move us in the direction of a more humanistic way of life, where there is care and concern about the well-being of us all.

First, let's recap the journey we have been on.

We came to understand what it's like to live from limiting beliefs and experiences, like the frogs in jars that stopped trying to jump out once the lids were removed.

We became aware of the messages and conditioning passed down through generations that shaped who we became and have kept us from being our true selves.

We have cultivated a more positive self-view.

We've become more resilient.

We now know what's possible for our relationships.

Our world will improve just like our relationships when we realize that each of us individually makes up the world. It's about what we bring to the world and who we are in the world. It's the people who create how the world is. Now you can take the progress you've made and expand it out into the world by being your confident, happy, resilient, self.

Words to Live By

Abundance

To have an abundance is to have more than you need, a great supply, more than enough. Someone with an abundant mentality is genuinely happy for others when they succeed.

Acceptance

To be in acceptance is to allow others to be their unique persons. That means having a right to their thoughts, feelings, and opinions. Acceptance does not mean agreement. When you accept people for who they are, you let go of your desire to change them.

Attentive

Paying close attention to something or someone and listening to or observing something is being attentive. So is being thoughtful of others, considerate, polite, and courteous.

Belonging

Being a member or part of a group or family is belonging. A sense of belonging is a human need, just like the need for food and shelter. Without belonging somewhere, people often feel isolated and lonely.

Caring

Feeling and showing concern, empathy, kindness, care, and compassion for others is caring. A caring person may offer help, emotional support, or look after those unable to care for themselves.

Collaboration

Collaboration involves individuals working together for a common purpose to create or achieve something. It's a joint effort between two or more people with a common goal or shared priority.

Community

Community is a feeling of fellowship with others as a result of sharing common attitudes, interests, and goals.

Compassion

The feeling that arises when confronted with another's suffering and feeling motivated to relieve that suffering is compassion. It's the feeling of wanting to help someone who is sick, hungry, or in trouble. It's also offering understanding and kindness to others when they fail or make mistakes, rather than judging them harshly.

Curiosity

Curiosity is a strong desire to know or learn something. It's also recognizing and seeking out novel and challenging information and experiences.

Deliberate

Doing something consciously and intentionally is being deliberate. So is thinking about or discussing issues and decisions carefully. Being deliberate is also to consider reasons for and against something to make up one's mind.

Generosity

Generosity is being kind and generous. It's a willingness to give or to share something, to give help or support. Someone showing generosity is happy to give time, money, food, or kindness to people in need.

Happiness

Happiness is a positive emotional state characterized by feelings such as contentment, joy, life satisfaction, fulfillment, and well-being.

Inclusion

The act of including someone or something as part of a group is inclusion. In a work setting, inclusion means that employees are respected, valued, recognized, appreciated, and supported, allowing them to utilize their talents, skills, and perspectives to reach their full potential while contributing to the business's success as a whole.

Interested

Being interested is having or showing an interest in something or someone. It's also being curious, fascinated, concerned, or wanting to know about something.

Kindness

Kindness is being friendly, gentle, and considerate, marked by acts of generosity, consideration, or concern for others without expecting praise or reward. It's also being helpful and caring about other people.

Loving

Being nurturing, warm, safe, and supportive are ways of being loving. So is going out of your way to make your partner, friend, or child's day special.

Receiving

To receive from another person is to accept things like a gift, money, or a compliment. Receiving means accepting offers of help, assistance, kindness, and generosity.

Respect

Respect is treating or thinking about someone with regard for their feelings, wishes, rights, or traditions. It's the ability to relate to others in ways that consider their priorities and ideas important.

Satisfaction

Satisfaction is the good feeling you have when you have achieved something, received something you wanted, or done something you wanted to do.

Serenity

Serenity is being calm, peaceful, and untroubled. It's the absence of mental stress or anxiety. The Serenity Prayer is: *God, grant me the serenity to accept the things I cannot change, the courage to change the things I can, and the wisdom to know the difference.*

Supportive

A supportive person is kind, caring, encouraging, understanding, reassuring, and helpful to someone embarking on something new or going through a difficult time. Emotional or financial support are two common ways to be supportive.

Unity

Unity is togetherness or oneness, united or joined as a whole. When people act as one and are on the same page, they display unity. Unity is the opposite of being divided.

Validation

Validation is the act of acknowledging what someone else is saying or feeling. Validation is essential for every relationship, including friendships, romantic relationships, and family members. Validation builds a sense of belonging and strengthens relationships. People often invalidate someone because they cannot process that person's emotions. They might be preoccupied with their own problems or not know how to respond at that moment.

Wisdom

Wisdom is using your knowledge and experience to make good judgments and decisions. It's also having insight and ability to discern or judge what is true, right, or lasting.

How to Use These Words

There are an unlimited number of ways to incorporate these words into your daily life and with your friends, family, and at your place of work. Here are some ideas to get you started:

Choose a word each day, week, or month to apply to your life or relationships.

Write each word on small separate pieces of paper. Then fold them and place them in a jar. Draw one word out of the jar as your "word of the day" or "word of the week."

Choose a word and do some journal writing about what that word means to you.

Meditate on a word.

Doodle or draw a design using a word as you think about its meaning and living by it.

Invite your partner and children to use these words as a guide to improve your family life.

Get a "buddy," group of friends, coworkers, or neighbors together to share these words with and live by them.

Choose a word and write it on several pieces of paper to place by your desk, on your bathroom mirror, and on your refrigerator as a reminder to stay aware of living by that word. Continue with that word until you're ready to select another one.

As I said at the beginning of the book, when enough of us replace the programming and conditioning we were raised with and embrace new ways of thinking, feeling, coping, and doing, we will see and experience positive changes in our families, workplaces, communities, schools, and everywhere else!

An Invitation

Leave a Review

Please consider leaving a review on Amazon or your favorite book site so others may find this book and benefit as well. If you would like to provide feedback, please email me at: phyllis@phyllisginsberg.com

Contact Me

Email: phyllis@phyllisginsberg.com
Website: www.phyllisginsberg.com
Facebook: www.facebook.com/phyllis.ginsberg
LinkedIn: www.linkedin.com/in/phyllisginsberg

Speaking and Interviews

To learn about booking Phyllis for speaking engagements,
workshops, retreats, or interviews, visit:
www.phyllisginsberg.com/media/#speak

Acknowledgments

First and foremost, I owe myself a huge acknowledgment for having the patience and determination to complete this book. I was almost done with it, or so I thought, and then I fell and broke my wrist. Not being able to type was a huge setback. I tried typing left-handed, and it was exhausting, especially trying to cut and paste sections and sentences.

I was put in a position to experience what this book is about!

The support from family, friends, fellow authors, and the incredible team at Capucia Publishing allowed me to put myself first and do what I needed to do for myself rather than focus on a deadline.

A big thank you goes to my daughter, Stephanie Ginsberg, who helped me rearrange the content of this book, making it a better reader experience. It was fun spending two weekend "retreats" together!

Ultimately, it's the people I have been fortunate to work with during my career that have given me the ability to use my knowledge, skills, gifts, and talents to make a difference in their lives and share them with you.

References

The American Academy of Child and Adolescent Psychiatry. "TV Violence and Children." 2017. 12 December. www.aacap.org/AACAP/Families_and_Youth/Facts_for_Families/FFF-Guide/Children-And-TV-Violence-013.aspx

Associated Press, 2020. "Americans are the unhappiest they've been in 50 years, poll finds." 30 July 2023. www.nbcnews.com/politics/politics-news/americans-are-unhappiest-they-ve-been-50-years-poll-finds-n1231153

Center on Developing Child, Harvard University. 2023. "Early Childhood Mental Health." 30 July 2023. www.developingchild.harvard.edu/science/deep-dives/mental-health

JAMA Pediatrics. 2019. "Positive Childhood Experiences and Adult Mental and Relational Health in a Statewide Sample: Associations Across Adverse Childhood Experiences Levels." 30 July 2023. www.jamanetwork.com/journals/jamapediatrics/fullarticle/2749336

K12 Academics. "History of School Shootings in the United States." 30 July 2023. www.k12academics.com/school-shootings/history-school-shootings-united-states

Maté, Gabor. 2022. *The Myth of Normal: Trauma, Illness, and Healing in a Toxic Culture*. New York City: Avery

Neff, Kristin. 2015. *Self-Compassion: Stop Beating Yourself Up and Leave Insecurity Behind*. New York City: William Morrow Paperbacks

Oberlo. 2023. "How Much Time Does the Average Person Spend on Social Media? (2012–2022)." 30 July 2023. www. oberlo.com/statistics/how-much-time-does-the-average-person-spend-on-social-media#:~:text=your%20free%20 trial-,Average%20time%20spent%20on%20social%20 media,also%20the%20highest%20ever%20recorded

Perry, Bruce and Winfrey, Oprah. 2021. *What Happened to You?* Flatiron Books: New York

Rubin, Gretchen. 2017. *The Four Tendencies*. New York: Harmony Books.

Saujani, Reshma. 2019. *Brave, Not Perfect: How Celebrating Imperfection Helps You Live Your Best, Most Joyful Life.* New York: Currency.

Simon, George. 2010. *In Sheep's Clothing: Understanding and Dealing with Manipulative People*. Michigan: Parkhurst

About the Author

Phyllis Ginsberg is a beacon of inspiration in the realm of personal transformation. She has an unwavering commitment to guiding individuals toward their true potential. With thirty-plus years as a seasoned marriage and family counselor and an unquenchable thirst for knowledge, Phyllis empowers her clients to break free from the constraints of their past and unleash the full power of their minds.

Phyllis has been a prominent figure in various esteemed platforms, including the impactful documentary "The Courage to Continue," *Woman's World* magazine, CNBC, *Parade* magazine, *Health & Wellbeing* magazine, and The Today Show Digital. As an international bestselling author and inspirational speaker, her influence leaves an enduring impact on the lives she touches.

At the heart of her transformative journey lies her acclaimed book, *Brain Makeover: A Weekly Guide to a Happier, Healthier, and*

More Abundant Life, which has garnered praise and recognition far and wide. Notably, CNBC contributor Steve Adcock attests to the profound influence of Phyllis' work in his ability to achieve both financial success and unwavering happiness.

With a strong commitment to empowering individuals, Phyllis' second book, *Tired and Hungry No More: Not Your Ordinary Guide to Reclaiming Your Health and Happiness*, stands as a testament to her holistic approach to well-being.

Affectionately known as the Survival to Thrival Expert, Phyllis sparks genuine transformation in the lives of countless individuals who yearn to rise above mere survival and thrive in the face of life's challenges. Her unique blend of wisdom, empathy, and actionable insights has earned her a cherished place in the hearts of those fortunate enough to cross her path.

Described as a guiding light, Phyllis Ginsberg has an undeniable impact. Her journey is a testament to the boundless potential of the human spirit. She is a leader in catalyzing personal transformation in our modern world. Her legacy of empowerment and growth remains an enduring source of inspiration.

Phyllis and her husband reside in the San Francisco Bay Area, where her presence continues to ripple through the lives she touches. To learn more about Phyllis' transformative work to embark on your own journey of growth or to book her to speak, visit www.phyllisginsberg.com.

Also by Phyllis Ginsberg

Brain Makeover: A Weekly Guide to a Happier, Healthier, and More Abundant Life is a number one international bestseller and has been featured in articles on CNBC, *Parade* magazine, *Health and Wellbeing* magazine, and *Women's World* magazine.

Tired and Hungry No More: Not Your Ordinary Guide to Reclaiming Your Health and Happiness

www.ingramcontent.com/pod-product-compliance
Lightning Source LLC
Chambersburg PA
CBHW070918120626
46546CB00001B/318